The Wedding
Sourcebook

The Wedding Sourcebook

by

Madeline Barillo

Lowell House
Los Angeles

Contemporary Books
Chicago

Library of Congress Cataloging-in-Publication Data

Barillo, Madeline.
    The wedding sourcebook / by Madeline Barillo.
        p.   cm.
    Includes bibliographical references and index.
    ISBN 1-56565-448-X
    1. Weddings—Planning.   2. Wedding etiquette.   I. Title.
  HQ748.B37   1996
  395'.22—dc20   95-43582
                                          CIP

Requests for such permissions should be addressed to:
Lowell House
2029 Century Park East, Suite 3290
Los Angeles, CA 90067

Lowell House books can be purchased at special discounts when ordered in bulk for premiums and special sales. Contact Department JH at the address above.

Publisher: Jack Artenstein
General Manager, Lowell House Adult: Bud Sperry
Managing Editor: Maria Magallanes
Text design: Laurie Young
Illustrations: Elisa Cohen

Manufactured in the United States of America
10 9 8 7 6 5 4 3 2 1

Acknowledgments

Special thanks to editors Cele Goldsmith Lalli and Mary Ann Cavlin, who have given me dream assignments over the years and always make me laugh.

To my husband, Gregory Flagg, for his love and encouragement, and for being a true Sensitive New Age Guy.

To my dearest friend Christiana Figueres, for flying in from Germany to be my lone bridesmaid (and dying her bridesmaid shoes midnight blue to make my mother happy).

To Lowell House editors Bud Sperry and Maria Magallanes, for their hard work and enthusiasm for this project, and Laurie Young and Elisa Cohen who did the handsome text design and illustrations.

And to all the brides, consultants, and wedding industry professionals who lent their expertise to this book, including Millie Martini Bratten, Patricia Bruneau, Michael Carter, Sandra Casolino, Reverend Roger Coleman, Linda DeMarkey, Beverly Dembo, Robbi Ernst III, Benita Foresta, Steve Freitag, Gaye Greenamyer, Earle Greenberg, Joel Greenberg, Michelle Hodges, Laura Torres Hodgins, Diane James, John Kozero, Cheryl Kremkow, Jodie LaMarre, Sandra Lefkowitz, Teddy Lenderman, Tref Lowe, Karen Lucas, Reverend Randy Mayeux, Paul McGuirk, Gerard Monaghan, Christine Morrissey, Elizabeth Mushinksy, Susan Regan, Michael Roman, Lyn Rosenfield, Andrea Eginton Seton, Doris Shulman, Jessica Siegel, Scott L. Smith, Shannon Smith, Annenna Sorenson, Wendy Stewart, Mikki Viereck, Joel Windham, Denise Winkelstein, Martine Sixto Wirtemburg, and Virginia Wolff.

Contents

Preface	Congratulations! You're Getting Married!	ix
Chapter One	We're Engaged	I
Chapter Two	It Begins with a Budget	23
Chapter Three	The Wedding Consultant	55
Chapter Four	The Bridal Gift Registry	67
Chapter Five	Wedding Parties and Showers	77
Chapter Six	Dressing the Bride and Attendants	87
Chapter Seven	The Wedding Cake	119
Chapter Eight	Flowers	131
Chapter Nine	Photography and Videography	145
Chapter Ten	Invitations and Accessories	159
Chapter Eleven	Children at the Wedding	179
Chapter Twelve	Wedding Ceremonies and Customs	185
Chapter Thirteen	Music for the Ceremony and Reception	213
Chapter Fourteen	The Reception and Catering	227
Chapter Fifteen	The Honeymoon	255
Chapter Sixteen	From Here to Matrimony: Wedding Stress, Preparation for Marriage, and How to Handle It All	269
Appendix		291
Index		311

Congratulations!
You're getting married!

Being engaged is an exciting time of discovery and celebration. It can be absolutely wonderful—full of romance and moments to savor. Some couples seem to float on a blissfully goofy cloud from the time one of them says, "I will," to the moment they both say, "I do!"

It can be a little overwhelming, too. Suddenly, the whole world treats you differently. Everybody loves lovers, the old saying goes. It's true. Once the word is out about the engagement, friends and family feel caught up in your excitement and volunteer their opinions. There are endless decisions to make, deadlines to meet, people to hire, and loved ones to include. Out of nowhere, your private relationship goes very public, your parents act as if it's *their* wedding, and it's easy to become consumed by the silliest details ("You mean the ribbons for the bouquets come in pinky peach, but not peachy salmon?").

Relax. This book was written to make it all more manageable and help brides and grooms actually enjoy the planning process. It is intended as a first-stop sourcebook and practical guide to wedding planning, to help make the journey down the aisle easier and stress free. Planning a wedding is a major undertaking, kind of like directing, producing, and starring in your own motion picture. Most couples have simply never organized such a big ceremony and party before, especially not for such a landmark moment in their lives.

Today, weddings in America are a $32 billion business. The average newlyweds spend $15,000 for a wedding and invite around two hundred guests. Couples no longer have the luxury of spare time to plan, since most couples are both working and the bride's mother, who traditionally helped with wedding arrangements, is probably working too. With all the effort, expense, and emotion that goes into planning something as important as a wedding, it's important to avoid costly mistakes.

My entrée into the "white gown" industry was unusual. I began writing wedding-planning articles more than twelve years ago while working as an editorial assistant for *The Advocate*, a daily city newspaper in Stamford, Connecticut. My job was basically to fetch coffee for reporters, type in the daily stock market quotes, and write obituaries.

One day, when a sympathetic editor named Stacy Schneider threw a bridal story my way, I grabbed it. I figured talking to giddy brides *had* to be better than verifying funeral arrangements with sobbing relatives.

It was. And it was irresistible. Engaged couples and their parents were cheerful and relentlessly optimistic. They were all eager to share their stories, and their joy was infectious.

Over the years, I've continued to cover bridal stories for *The Advocate* and the *Greenwich Time* newspaper in Greenwich, Connecticut. I've also done graduate work in marriage and family therapy and am a regular contributor to *Modern Bride* magazine. Last year, I began teaching The Perfect Wedding, a wedding-planning course at Norwalk Community-Technical College in Norwalk, Connecticut, where I work as a staff writer.

The Wedding Sourcebook was designed to provide a compendium of all the important deadlines and details engaged couples need to know, including what questions to ask before hiring vendors, easy-to-read checklists, traditional wedding etiquette, where to go for more information, and successful strategies from real couples. It also features expert advice from wedding industry professionals, including consultants, etiquette experts, clergy, florists, photographers, musicians, caterers, and even parents and wedding guests.

Use it to make the wedding you've always dreamed of. And may every day of marriage be as special as your wedding day.

—Madeline Barillo

This book is dedicated to my daughters,

Alexandra and Victoria Flagg

The Wedding
Sourcebook

Chapter One

We're Engaged!

Every engagement begins with a proposal.
Who proposed to whom?

The wedding proposal is probably one of the most romantic notions in popular culture. No matter where or how it takes place, it's the grand gesture that means two people have chosen to make a lifelong bond to each other—a commitment intended to last, no matter what kind of curve balls life throws their way.

My husband proposed over the telephone when I was living in Germany and he was back home in the States. The 5 A.M. transatlantic call was hardly the stuff of a Danielle Steele novel (he woke me up and I was cranky), but to us it was romantic and memorable.

While covering wedding planning over the years for a daily city newspaper, I've interviewed couples who've gotten engaged in all sorts of places. Some came to a mutual, businesslike agreement over a cup of coffee or decided after years of living together to opt for the legal ceremony and license.

Others did it with a bit more flourish, like the groom-to-be who had his message carved into the stones of a park footpath in Connecticut and strolled with his girlfriend from step to step until she landed on WILL YOU MARRY ME? (The minute she said yes, they celebrated with champagne he'd stashed in a bucket under a bush.) Another would-be groom popped the question high above the Massachusetts countryside in a hot-air balloon, while another tucked his proposal into a Chinese fortune cookie. He'd shrunk the message to lilliputian size by reducing it time and again on a copying machine. (The poor fellow almost fainted when his girlfriend decided to pass up dessert and asked the waiter to clear the cookies away.) One gallant guy even proposed on traditional bended knee, velvet ring box in one hand and bouquet of red roses in the other.

SHARING THE GOOD NEWS

Until recently, it was customary for the groom to ask the bride's father for her hand in marriage. (Dad had to say yes before his daughter got to do the same.) The tradition was rooted in the days when a bride was considered a true piece of property and marriages were often arranged. The marriage proposal was a sort of business transaction involving a bride, a groom, and a dowry—which was literally a form of payment to the groom for taking a daughter off her father's hands.

In some cultures even today, the dowry is still ceremonially observed in the form of the bride's family paying for the wedding or the literal exchange of goats, chickens, or livestock.

These days, since marriages are self-arranged and the groom isn't expected to formally ask for the bride's hand, it's a special courtesy to make the engagement announcement to the bride's parents in person. If the parents don't live close by, try to arrange a conference call where everyone is on the phone line. If the parents are divorced, visit one parent first (usually the parent who raised you or is closest to you), and then the other.

The groom's parents are notified next. Some grooms prefer to tell their own parents privately. Again, it's better to do it in person, but a long-distance conference call will also do.

Once the groom's parents are notified, they traditionally call on the bride's parents. A phone call or visit is always welcome and sets the tone for a future warm relationship. If the groom's parents don't make the first move, don't stand on ceremony. The bride's parents may contact them.

It's a nice touch to arrange for the future in-laws to meet in person and get to know each other as soon as possible before the wedding. This is an important gesture. In our society, couples are generally more mobile and better educated than ever before. Unlike the days when most people met and married in their own hometown, couples today often fall in love far from home and meet at school, at work, or at the nearby cappuccino bar. Forget the image of the boy marrying the girl next door or a hometown sweetheart. Chances are greater than ever that your parents may never have laid eyes on your intended.

3

Special Considerations

If one or both of you has children, you will want to tell them about the impending marriage first—before they hear about it from anyone else. Make the announcement in a place where the kids feel safe and comfortable—like home sweet home—and where they can freely express any anxieties or fears.

Even grown children may have strong reactions to the idea of a new step-parent. It's important to reassure children about the ways in which their lives will stay the same after the marriage (they already know life will change in some ways!) and the fact that your love for them won't be diminished.

Also, if you have a former spouse (and are on speaking terms), communicate directly to him or her about your plans. *Never* use a child to relay that kind of emotionally charged information! It puts the child in a difficult and uncomfortable position and can create serious loyalty conflicts. A simple note or phone call to the former spouse will also do. But if you feel your ex might actually disrupt the wedding plans, don't feel compelled to tell him or her about the wedding at all.

If you are remarrying following the death of a spouse and feel the news might be painful to your former in-laws, be sure to notify them in person or via personal note. Spare them hearing it from someone else. Your marriage, no matter how much joy it might bring them, could also be considered the final severing of an important tie to their deceased child.

LET THE CELEBRATING BEGIN!

Some couples prefer to make a dramatic public announcement of the good news when close family and friends are all together at an engagement party. The engagement party is traditionally hosted by the bride's parents, but anyone can give one and it's not uncommon these days for the couple to host one themselves. This is a wonderful time for both families and friends of the bride and groom to meet.

An engagement celebration is usually an informal affair—a brunch, luncheon, dinner, picnic, or cocktail party held in a private home or restaurant. Formal invitations are seldom necessary.

Years ago, the engagement announcement was traditionally made at the party during a formal toast given by the bride's father. Since the announcement was usually a surprise to most of the guests, gifts were not expected. (If guests do arrive with gifts, it's thoughtful to set them aside and open them privately later.)

Now is the time to get in the habit of writing a thank-you note promptly after receiving a gift! Notes should be written within a day of receiving the gift. It's also a gracious touch to thank the party hosts with a note or a gift of flowers.

While on the subject of note writing, remember that every engagement or wedding gift should be acknowledged with a personal note—the sooner the better, and certainly not a moment past three months. Anyone who took the time to choose something special for you deserves some sort of acknowledgment and will appreciate knowing it arrived safe and sound. The traditional standard is for hand-written notes (not mass-produced printed ones) written on fine-quality plain or engraved paper or informal cards. Thank-you notes need not be tomes. A few sentences acknowledging the gift and what you plan to do with it are fine: "Dear Aunt Mary, the wine goblets you sent us are lovely. Perhaps you will join us for dinner sometime after the wedding and see for yourself how handsome they look on our table." Thank-you notes were once

5

written exclusively by the bride, even if the wedding gift was addressed to the groom or from someone the bride had never met. Thankfully, grooms are now sharing the task!

Did You Know . . . ?

- A couple is officially engaged the moment both agree to marry. No ring is necessary for it to be "official."

- If the engagement announcement will be a surprise to the guests, the party invitation should not refer to the couple.

- If the party isn't a surprise to guests and formal invitations will be sent, the wording may read something like "You are invited to a brunch [dinner, cocktail party, etc.] in honor of Gina Davies and Stephen Freitag." Note that the bride's name goes first. An alternative wording is "Please join us in celebrating the engagement of Gina Davies and Stephen Freitag."

- The average length of an engagement today is fifteen months, notes Cele Lalli, editor-in-chief of *Modern Bride* magazine in *Modern Bride Guide to Etiquette.* This book is a terrific resource for any wedding-etiquette question, from wording the invitations to seating the guests at the reception.

- There is no "appropriate" length of time for an engagement. Some couples prefer a long engagement so they can both finish school or military service or save up for a new home.

Others opt for a whirlwind engagement of a few months or
weeks. (Marriage and family therapists, however, note that an
engagement of more than three years may signify somebody's
serious doubts.) This is a most personal decision, something
with which both of you should be comfortable.

❀ If the engagement is broken, you must notify everyone, but
there's no pressing need to share your reason or tell the whole
story. If a newspaper carried your engagement announcement, send in a new one along the lines of: "The engagement
of Martha Washington and Aaron Spelling has been canceled
by mutual consent." If invitations were already sent to guests,
have cards printed up that read "Mr. and Mrs. George
Washington announce that the marriage of their daughter
Martha to Aaron Spelling has been canceled." If wedding
invitations have not been mailed, you or members of your
close family can call or write guests to notify them.

Some wedding experts insist the engagement ring must be returned to the
former fiancé unless it was an heirloom from the bride's family, whether it was
reset or not. Others take the Joan Rivers route and advise the bride to hold
onto the ring if the man broke the engagement (after all, it was a gift to *her*) but
return it if she was the one who called it quits. And yes, all the engagement
gifts should be returned. (Which means don't be tempted to use them before
the wedding!)

THE NEWSPAPER ANNOUNCEMENTS

Placing an engagement and/or wedding announcement in the local newspaper makes for a lovely keepsake memento and also spreads the news to a wider circle of friends in the community.

You may place announcements in both your and your fiancé's hometown newspapers and in the towns where you live or work. This service is usually free.

Most newspapers have their own standard format to follow and will provide free forms to fill out. Call ahead to the paper's society, features, or community editor to request the forms (or simply clip the bridal pages in the paper and mimic the format).

Be sure to ask the editor about deadlines and what size and kind of photographs they will use. Most papers will run an engagement announcement anytime up to six weeks prior to the wedding date. Submit a wedding announcement two to four weeks before the wedding, or up to three months after the wedding.

Generally, newspapers will accept only black-and-white photos. These need not be professionally produced, but a clear, sharp image is crucial. Sometimes the photos can be returned if you supply a stamped, self-addressed envelope. Be sure to write your name *clearly* on a label on the back of the photo. (Never write directly on a photo, because the writing may smudge or bleed through into the image.) Always include daytime and evening phone numbers so that the paper can verify the information.

If space allows, some newspapers will include more than the bread-and-butter facts, such as prominent relatives of the bride or groom or interesting or newsworthy achievements ("The bride is the granddaughter of John Doe, who invented the first patent leather shoes and became a millionaire by the age of 18.") I remember the Greenwich, Connecticut, bride who asked that her dog's picture run with her engagement announcement in *Greenwich Time*. It seems the groom had given her a dog instead of a diamond as an engagement "ring." Some publications still include detailed descriptions of the bride's wedding gown and flowers. Often the bridal shop where you purchased the gown will supply a written description of the gown for you.

Did You Know . . . ?

❀ In any newspaper announcement, the bride's intended is always referred to as the "bridegroom" and not the "groom." That's because technically a groom refers to someone who tends horses!

Special Wordings

❀ When the parents are divorced, list them both, and if the mother is remarried, include her married name: "Mrs. Jane Riley of Tarrytown, New York, and Mr. John Besser of Ocean Grove, New Jersey, announce the engagement of their daughter, Melissa Besser, to . . ."

❀ When one parent is deceased: "Mrs. Judy Vincent has announced the engagement of her daughter, Miranda Vincent, to Clark Kent. Miss Vincent is also the daughter of the late Victor Vincent."

❀ When both parents are deceased, the announcement may be made by a close relative or the couple themselves.

(See the appendix for etiquette books geared to invitations and announcements.)

NEWSPAPER WEDDING ANNOUNCEMENT
SAMPLE WORKSHEET

Please type or print!

Photos must be black-and-white only.

Mail or fax to:

Community Life Editor
The Daily Planet
Clark Kent Lane
Metropolis, NY 12345

Bride's name _____

Bride's parents' names and town of residence _____

_____

Telephone (day)_____ (evening)_____

Bridegroom's name _____

Bridegroom's parents' names and town of residence _____

_____

Wedding date _____ Time _____ Place _____

Reception was held at _____

Officiating clergy _____

Matron or maid of honor's name (circle one) _____

Matron or maid of honor's hometown _____

Bridesmaids and their hometowns _____

_____

Best man _____ Hometown _____

Groomsmen and their hometowns _____

_____

Bride's occupation _____Where employed _____

Bridegroom's occupation _____Where employed _____

Schools and colleges (indicate if graduated; degrees)

Bride _____

Groom _____

Occupations of both sets of parents (indicate if retired) _____

_____

Honeymoon was spent _____

Couple now resides in _____

This information may be confirmed by calling (relation to bride or groom)

_____

Signed _____

Daytime phone number _____

11

NEWSPAPER ENGAGEMENT ANNOUNCEMENT
SAMPLE WORKSHEET

Please type or print!

Mail or fax to:

Community Life Editor
The Daily Planet
Clark Kent Lane
Metropolis, NY 12345

Full name of engaged woman _____

Telephone number (day) _____ (evening) _____

Address _____

Names and address of parents _____

_____

Schools and colleges (indicate if graduated; degrees)_____

_____

Occupation _____ Where employed _____

Date of wedding _____

Full name of fiancé _____

Address _____

Names and address of parents _____

_____

Schools and colleges (indicate if graduated) _____

_____

Occupation _____ Where employed _____

Additional information _____

This information may be confirmed by calling _____

Relation to engaged woman is _____

Signed _____

CHOOSING THE RINGS

It isn't written in stone that an engaged woman must wear a diamond ring—but most do. "About 82 percent of couples get an engagement ring when they get married, and most choose a diamond: almost 100 percent," notes Michael Roman, chairman of the board of the Jewelers of America, Inc., in New York City. "Initially, when you thought of a diamond, you thought of a round diamond. Now you get diamonds in various shapes, from an oval to a marquis to a pear shape, even a heart shape, and, of course, the emerald cut."

What determines the value of a diamond? The stones are judged by a standard that jewelers refer to as the four C's: carat weight, color, clarity, and cut. According to the brochure, *What You Should Know About Buying a Diamond* published by the Jewelers of America, they mean the following things:

Carat. The unit of weight used for diamonds. The word derives from the carob seeds used to balance scales in ancient times. There are 100 points to a carat, so a 99-point diamond weighs virtually 1 carat, and a 45-point diamond weighs a little less than half a carat.

Color. Grading a cut stone for color means deciding the amount by which it deviates from the whitest possible. Completely white (truly colorless) diamonds are rare, and therefore most valuable. Although most diamonds are a shade of white, diamonds come in all colors, including blue (like the Hope diamond), pale yellow, canary yellow, pink, red, green, and even brown. Colored diamonds (called "fancies") are prized for their depth of color, just as white diamonds are valued for their lack of color.

Clarity. Nature makes each stone unique. Some contain more imperfections (called "inclusions") than others. The fewer inclusions, the more valuable the diamond. A diamond's clarity is determined by taking into account the size, nature, and placement of these imperfections. (Keep in mind that slight flaws cannot be detected by the naked eye and don't affect a stone's beauty.)

Cut. Diamonds are cut by skilled craftsmen according to a mathematical formula. A finished diamond has 58 facets, which are the small, flat, polished planes cut into the stone so that the maximum amount of light is reflected. This reflection, called "brilliance," is important in evaluating a diamond's quality, since accuracy in cutting is essential to the diamond's beauty. More than half of all couples choose the round brilliant cut.

How much should you spend on an engagement ring? The rule of thumb is to set aside two months' salary on the ring, but this is a personal decision.

Think carefully about buying a ring for "investment purposes" or resale value. How many couples do you know who have *actually* sold their diamond, even in the face of personal financial crisis?

Look for a ring that fits properly. It should slip comfortably over the knuckle and hug the base of the finger without sliding around too easily. Since hands swell slightly in warm weather, keep the "toothpick" rule in mind, and allow for enough room for a toothpick to fit between the ring and the finger.

Insure your ring as soon as possible, either on a homeowner's or renter's policy. Keep copies of all receipts in a safe place. That way, all's not lost forever if you accidentally drop it down the sink.

Many couples now favor wedding and engagement rings designed to look like one ring. These new sets may be interlocking pairs or designed to fit side by side.

Gemstones

For the bride who wants a unique ring, colored gemstones are becoming a popular option. When Prince Charles of England proposed to Lady Diana Spencer, he gave her a stunning blue sapphire ring surrounded by diamonds. Actress Jane Fonda wore an opal-and-diamond engagement ring when she married media mogul Ted Turner.

Over the centuries, gemstones have been prized for their beauty as well as their romantic folklore. Green emeralds were believed to ensure lasting love, rubies were associated with health and passion, sapphires symbolized sincerity and fidelity, opals represented hope and purity.

"A woman should really love a ring she will wear every day for the rest of her

15

life," says Cheryl Kremkow, director of the Gembureau, a gemstone information service in New York City. "Gemstones are among the most individual of nature's creations: perfect crystals in every color of the rainbow, with no two alike."

The Gembureau notes that until a few hundred years ago, color was the way gemstones were identified: all red gems were called ruby, all blue gems, sapphire, and all green gems, emerald or jade. But thanks to gemology (the scientific study of gems), we can now identify different varieties of gemstones in all manner of colors. The bonus for brides is that many of these gems are not necessarily rare and are in less demand, and therefore much less expensive than such better-known stones as emeralds, sapphires, and rubies.

Exciting new gem discoveries include tourmalines, garnets, spinels, tanzanites, aquamarines, iolites, amethysts, citrines, peridots, and topaz. You may have seen these gemstones featured in jewelry sold on the shop-at-home television networks.

Like diamonds, gemstones are evaluated according to the four C's: carat weight, color, clarity, and cut. Stones with muted colors or colors between hues are generally less expensive than those with clear primary colors.

Did you know sapphires come in red, pink, orange, green, violet, and yellow, as well as royal blue?

The Gembureau notes other colors in the gemstone rainbow:

Red: ruby, garnet, spinel, alexandrite

Pink: ruby, sapphire, garnet, kunzite, topaz

Orange: sapphire, garnet, citrine, spinel, topaz, zircon, tourmaline, and fire opal

Violet: amethyst, garnet, sapphire, tourmaline, jadeite

Green: emerald, peridot, sapphire, nephrite, tsavorite garnet, and chrysoberyl

Blue: sapphire, aquamarine, spinel, iolite, lapis lazuli, and topaz

Yellow/Gold: sapphire, citrine, golden beryl, amber, garnet, and alusite

When Selecting a Gemstone or Diamond Engagement Ring . . .

❀ Choose a reputable store that has been in business a long time and that offers a large selection at many price points. "You get what you pay for," notes Joel Windham, general counsel for the Jewelers' Vigilance Committee in New York City, a national nonprofit trade association. "We suggest dealing with someone you trust. A 'bargain of a lifetime' is your first red flag."

❀ Buy the best-quality stone you can afford.

❀ Keep in mind that some gemstones are more durable than others. Sapphires, according to the Gembureau, are perhaps the toughest and most durable.

17

- Before you purchase a stone, have its four C's (carat weight, color, clarity, and cut) certified.

- Ask about the retailer's return policy and whether there is an extra charge for sizing the ring.

- Have the jewelry appraised by an independent and reputable gemologist, one not recommended by the jeweler, advises *Avoiding the Wedding Bell Blues,* published by the New York City Department of Consumer Affairs. Be aware that appraisals can vary as much as 25 percent.

- Keep all receipts and pay by credit card. That way you'll have more legal recourse and can withhold payment until a problem is settled.

- If you have a problem or feel the jeweler has made fraudulent claims about the stone, file a *written* complaint with all of the following:

> The Department of Consumer Affairs
> Complaint Division
> 42 Broadway
> New York, NY 10004
> *(or the local consumer affairs division in*
> *your own state)*

> The Jewelers' Vigilance Committee
> 401 E. 34th St., Suite N 13A
> New York, NY 10016

> The Better Business Bureau in your area.

"The wedding and engagement announcements we get are true reflections of the times—divorced parents, dual-career couples, deadbeat dads, second marriages, older brides. I can't tell you how many times the father of the bride or groom has been left off an announcement and when we call to get the father's name are told to leave him out—'He ran off many years ago and we haven't heard from him since.' Many couples are products of divorces, often on both sides, and many times a girl's engagement is announced by two sets of parents—mother, father, and both their new spouses. One time a very prim, upper-crust woman came in with an announcement for her daughter and fiancé and told me rather disapprovingly, 'They're living in sin, you know.' I consoled her by telling her, 'So am I.' When it comes to weddings today, anything goes. We've seen mothers giving the bride away, two or more best men, and a woman who stood up as best man. So far we haven't gotten any male brides-maids, but I'm sure that's next."

—Susan Regan, assistant features editor, *Greenwich Time* newspaper

TOP WEDDING MYTHS

1. **Only virgins should wear a white wedding gown.**

   White dresses became popular only after Queen Victoria wore one in the 1840s. White symbolizes different things in different cultures: joy, fertility, or virginity. Anyone can wear a white wedding gown.

2. **If you don't wear a diamond ring, you aren't officially engaged.**

   Nonsense. An engagement is official as soon as a couple declare their intention to marry. No ring is needed, and it needn't be a diamond. Paper cigar bands have even filled in quite nicely for some couples.

3. **The bride's family always pays for the wedding.**

   Here's good news for the bride's family: Tradition once dictated that they paid for the whole enchilada, but not anymore. These days, couples are paying for all or part of the wedding themselves, and any relatives may chip in.

4. **A wedding reception must include a meal.**

   A wedding reception is a celebration, and not every celebration includes a huge meal. For an informal wedding or an intimate late-night gathering, a wedding cake and simple refreshments are fine.

5. **You can't say no to being a bridesmaid.**

   Sure you can! An invitation to be a bridesmaid is an honor, but it also carries a price tag. The commitment involves time and often the cost of wedding attire and transportation to the wedding. If this is a financial burden, it's appropriate to say, "Thank you, I'm honored, but it's just not possible for me right now. May I participate in another way, perhaps helping with the wedding planning?" A thoughtful bride will understand and *not* feel rejected.

6. **Only the bride's father can walk her down the aisle or give her away.**

   If the bride's father is deceased or played a minor role in her life because of divorce or other reasons, she can choose to "give" herself to her new husband, or else a mother, friend, or loved one can do the honor.

7. **There should always be an equal number of bridesmaids and ushers.**

   Not necessarily (although it looks balanced in pictures). Surround yourself with the people you care about, even if that means eight ushers and one bridesmaid.

8. **If the groom has sisters, the bride must include them in the wedding party.**

   Although it's a loving gesture to invite a future sister-in-law to stand up for you, it's not mandatory. (The wedding police are not going to come and take you away.) And there is no pressing need to explain why you have chosen other friends or relatives instead of her. If you feel guilty or awkward, involve her in some other way.

9. **Older brides can't wear a long gown.**

   A bride of any age can wear any gown she chooses, as long as it makes her feel lovely.

10. **A bride marrying for the second time can't wear a long gown.**

    Wrong again! We repeat: A bride can wear any gown she chooses, as long as it makes her feel lovely. This may be a remarriage, but unless you are marrying the same man the second time around, it's the first wedding for the two of you.

11. **Gifts of money are always considered tacky.**

    In some cultures, gifts of money are appropriate and expected. The gift is intended to help the couple get financially established.

12. **There must be a receiving line.**

    A receiving line makes it easier to greet each guest and thank him or her for coming, but you can choose to forgo the tradition. Just be sure to say a few words of thanks at the reception.

13. **Wedding cakes are always tiered.**

    Not anymore. The trend is toward cakes that taste as good as they look. Cakes may be single layers or multiple single layers displayed on a table.

21

14. **Members of the bride's family cannot give her a shower.**

    It was once considered crass for the bride's mother or sister to give her a shower, but this tradition has yielded. Now anyone who wants to fete the bride or couple can do so. Let the parties begin!

15. **Whoever catches the bouquet keeps it.**

    The bride may ask for her bouquet back in order to preserve it or press it. If you feel uncomfortable asking for it after the toss, arrange for the florist to make up a separate bouquet just for throwing.

16. **Invitations should be engraved and on white folded paper.**

    Engraved invitations are still the standard for the ultraformal wedding, but many couples are opting for the less expensive thermography printing method. And these days, colored and highly decorated invitations are gaining favor.

17. **An invitation to a wedding means an obligation to send a gift.**

    Only if you accept the invitation and attend the wedding.

Chapter Two

It Begins with a Budget

Planning a wedding can be exciting or excruciating.

Unless you're a seasoned hostess or professional event planner, the prospect of throwing a party for a hundred or more people is challenging—kind of like directing, producing, and starring in your own major motion picture.

WHERE TO BEGIN?

The first step is to think carefully about the kind of wedding *you* really want. Some brides have secretly nurtured a fantasy about their wedding since childhood. And all couples have conscious or unconscious notions about what a wedding should be or should include.

It all has to do with expectations and what we've grown up believing and treasuring about wedding customs and ceremonies. These are powerful notions that can create stress when, for instance, halfway through the planning the groom announces his relatives always expect party favors at a reception, but the bride thinks the idea is awful.

To really think through what you want and expect from your wedding and ceremony, try a visualization exercise. (For a moment, forget about time constraints or budget considerations. This is your fantasy, and you can do anything you want with it!) Close your eyes. Imagine your wedding day. What are you wearing? Where are you? How are you feeling? What is the ceremony like? What does it sound like and look like? Who is with you? How are they dressed?

Now you are at the reception. Where is it being held? What is it like? Are there many people around you, or an intimate group? What is the music like? What foods are you enjoying with family and friends? What kind of a celebration is it? What is the overall feeling of the moment?

Visualizing the wedding you want can be an enormously valuable step toward clarifying your expectations and expressing them out loud to your fiancé. Don't expect your partner to be a mind reader! How could he possibly know you've always wanted to wear a tea-length wedding dress and arrive in a horse-drawn carriage if you've never told him?

Since parents often play a powerful role in wedding planning—whether or not they are contributing financially—ask them to try the visualization exercise too. Then ask each of them to describe their own scenario. Parents often muse about their child's wedding from the moment the baby is born.

Now is the time to realize that weddings are a special crazy-quilt kind of celebration: two individuals meet for a very personal celebration of their very private bond, usually in a very public place with loads of people looking on. What's more, the bride and groom are contemporary people coming together for a ceremony steeped in centuries-old customs.

Forget about believing that this wedding is exclusively "yours." The very fact of asking loved ones to surround you on that day draws in a whole cast of characters who will have lots of opinions on how it should proceed. (And goodness, they will voice them.) Expect advice, advice, and more advice on everything from the choice of dinner mints to the ballet slippers worn by the littlest flower girl. Parents especially want to feel involved and make decisions—get ready for this one when they want to include old friends you've never even *met*. Yet at the same time, a couple should feel empowered to make their own decisions and generally steer the ship.

Power struggles often arise in the earliest stages of wedding planning because the centuries-old tradition that the bride's family pays for the wedding is no longer the standard.

Today, couples often pay for all or part of the wedding themselves, and since the "who pays for what" etiquette is getting fuzzier all the time, it's difficult for participants to know what's expected of them.

Often, he (or she) who pays for the wedding feels entitled to make the

25

rules. This is one of the stickiest aspects of contemporary wedding planning, so it's important to openly discuss with family members who will contribute what and when.

A good way to do this is to invite both sets of parents together for a casual dinner. Privately broach the budget subject to them beforehand. That way, those concerned arrive with a clear idea of what they can comfortably afford to do, and no one gets put on the spot.

Money is a sensitive issue for most people. It's important to be honest with yourself about the financial considerations and not cause undue burden for anyone. No couple should feel pressured to take on debt for a splashy wedding just when they are launching a new married life.

"We always advise our clients to realize that planning a wedding will often be a series of compromises," says Denise Winkelstein, a wedding and event consultant whose firm, Accents, is based in San Mateo, California. "The bride and groom must be up front with their families about their ideas for their wedding. Likewise, parents need to be up front about exactly how much money is available for the event."

Winkelstein advises clients to involve their families by assigning them specific responsibilities and tasks. Say, his mom scouts sites for the rehearsal dinner; your mom checks out prices on table linens and centerpieces.

Once you've got that "dream" wedding visualized and a budget firmly established, it's time to determine if compromise is called for. A professional wedding consultant can suggest ways to make easy trade-offs without your feeling deprived. It may mean trimming the guest list, scaling down the reception, or choosing pretty but more modestly priced flowers.

"There are some areas where you can be more flexible with your budget and others where you cannot," says Robbi Ernst III of June Wedding, Inc.® in Temple, Texas. A consultant and bridal industry educator, Ernst, dubbed the Cecil B. DeMille of weddings by the *Wall Street Journal*, notes that services like photography, music, and invitations are pretty much evenly priced, but a wedding budget can be easily thrown out of whack by items like catering and flowers. Catering represents up to half of average wedding costs, and flowers soak up another 10 percent (see pie chart). "That is where people can really go way over their budget, because prices vary *so* much," Ernst notes. Two strands of lily of the valley, for example, will cost you what fifty strands of carnations go for.

A wedding consultant can actually save a couple time and money, because these seasoned professionals have a working knowledge of what services cost and how a theme or special effect can be achieved on a shoestring budget (for more on wedding and event planners, read the following chapter on consultants).

Wedding consultant Pat Bruneau, of L'Affaire Du Temps in Milpitas, California, says couples often have unrealistic expectations about reception costs because they've simply never planned a large-scale party before and have no conception of what key services run. When a couple with a $4,000 limit asked her to plan a large wedding with expensive dinner buffet, fine wines, flowers, video, and all the trimmings, Bruneau had to diplomatically explain that the money simply wouldn't stretch that far. Instead, she showed them how to invite everybody without plunging into debt. Since the couple's priorities were a romantic setting and special event, Bruneau suggested a midafternoon cake-and-champagne reception featuring impressive keepsake favors (crystal perfume bottles), fine champagne, and a spectacular wedding cake.

27

"Instead of putting the money into so-so food, put it into an incredible cake, something just *wonderful*," she says. "The guests will walk away saying, 'What a beautiful setting; the cake was marvelous, and the favor was unique!'"

GETTING STARTED: AN EXPECTATIONS WORKSHEET

- What kind of wedding do *we* want? Circle how many apply: formal? ultraformal? casual? daytime or evening? special site? intimate? traditional? themed? destination wedding? offbeat or unusual?

- How does this image correspond to what others will want and expect for us?

- What possible conflicts may crop up?

- What do we *most* want people to remember about our wedding? (The food? backdrop? music? location? flowers?)

- How many guests do we hope to include?

- How much can we afford to spend overall?

- What kind of ceremony do we want——civil? religious? secular written by us?

- What special element(s) mean the most to us or are we willing to splurge on?

- What element(s) are we willing to cut corners on?

- What kind of financial assistance can we reasonably expect from parents or others?

❀ What other kinds of help can we expect from friends or loved ones (baking the cake, help with addressing invitations, help with making calls to vendors, and so on)?

❀ Which of your friends have recently gotten married and can offer practical advice?

❀ Whose wedding have we attended that most closely matches the one we envision for ourselves?

"A lot of people leave wedding planning to the last minute, but not me! I started planning a year and a half before. You can do a lot ahead if you have a general idea of the number of guests.

On the first day, I went to the church for a date, and then worked with the halls for a reception site. Eight months before the wedding, I had my invitations ready and printed so I could do them leisurely at home. I ordered the favors three months ahead—candy dishes and napkin holders. I ordered the gown to have by November (for a July wedding). Now I have time for fittings, and everything else is all done! You can relax if you are organized."

—Sandra Casolino, Connecticut July bride

Bride and Groom's Planning Calendar

Twelve to Eighteen Months Before

- ❑ Select an engagement ring (see chapter 1).

- ❑ Announce your engagement in the newspapers.

- ❑ Have engagement photograph taken (see chapter 9).

- ❑ Discuss wedding style, level of formality, time of day, and size with fiancé.

- ❑ Meet with clergy; reserve church or ceremony site (see chapter 12).

- ❑ Plan a meeting with fiancé and both sets of parents to openly discuss wedding expectations, costs, and responsibilities.

- ❑ Buy a calendar and loose-leaf notebook (or accordion file) to record wedding plans, important phone numbers, fabric swatches, and vendor contracts.

- ❑ Book a reception site. Find out if catering, cake, entertainment, flowers, linens, or other services are included.

- ❑ Discuss with fiancé the possibility of hiring an event planner or wedding consultant. Interview several (see chapter 3).

- ❑ Interview florists, photographers, videographers, musicians, caterers, and other wedding professionals. Book their services. Discuss deposits and cancellation clauses.

- ❑ Invite attendants to be in your wedding.

Nine Months Before

- [ ] Register for china, linens, crystal, and so on.

- [ ] Shop for wedding dress, headpiece, veil, and accessories.

- [ ] Discuss honeymoon plans and make reservations. If traveling abroad, research whether you'll need a passport, inoculations, and/or visa. If marrying abroad, contact a consulate office of that country here in the United States. Find out what the legal requirements are and what kinds of documents, waiting periods, or residency requirements are necessary (see chapter 15).

- [ ] Meet with bridesmaids to select their attire.

- [ ] Buy an index card file and record gifts, when they were received, and when thank-you notes were written. This file system comes in handy when it's time to address invitations and record acceptances.

- [ ] Ask both families to compile preliminary guest lists, including relationship (friend, uncle, etc.), current addresses, and phone/fax numbers.

Six Months Before

- ❑ Order wedding gown and accessories.

- ❑ Choose and order men's attire.

- ❑ Draw up final guest list; write each guest name, address, and response on a 3-by-5-inch file card. Keep writing thank-you notes!

- ❑ Select and order invitations (see chapter 10).

- ❑ Order personal stationery for writing letters and thank-you notes.

- ❑ Start thinking about the rehearsal dinner.

- ❑ Order bridesmaid gowns and accessories. If dyeing shoes to match, be sure all pairs are tinted at the same time in the same dye lot (even if it means the bridesmaids all ship their shoes to the same store for dyeing).

- ❑ Have both mothers select their dresses. The bride's mother traditionally chooses her ensemble first; the groom's mother then chooses a dress similar in formality and in a complementary color. (Remember, in wedding photographs they will be standing shoulder to shoulder with the bride, groom, and attendants, and you want the total look to be harmonious.)

- ❑ If desired, hire a calligrapher or arrange for computerized calligraphic services. If envelopes are available, save time by addressing them before the invitations arrive.

Four Months Before

- ❑ Decide where the two of you will live and order furnishings.

- ❑ Select and order invitations. Decide if you want to order a wedding "program" listing the attendants, ceremony music, liturgy, and so on.

- ❑ Prepare accurate direction sheets and maps for inclusion with invitations.

- ❑ Reserve rooms at a hotel for out-of-town guests; ask about discounts for wedding groups. Guests who will be making a weekend or getaway vacation will appreciate a list of local restaurants, transportation timetables, and attractions.

- ❑ Confirm that attire for bride, groom, attendants, and parents has been ordered. Confirm delivery dates. Keep the contracts on file!

- ❑ Shop for trousseau and clothing for prewedding parties.

- ❑ Order wedding rings (see chapter 1).

- ❑ Plan rehearsal dinner: time, date, menu, guest list.

- ❑ Make "tasting" session appointments with caterer and baker to sample wedding menu and wedding cake. Record choices on contract.

- ❑ Select an organist or soloist for wedding ceremony.

- ❑ Select ceremony liturgy and music (see chapter 13).

Two Months Before

- ❑ Check requirements for medical tests and marriage license.

- ❑ Mail wedding invitations at least four to eight weeks before wedding.

- ❑ Plan luncheon or special party for bridesmaids.

- ❑ Choose gifts for attendants and future spouse.

- ❑ Arrange for bridal portrait to be taken two to four weeks before wedding.

- ❑ Pick up wedding rings and check engraving.

- ❑ Meet with musicians or band leader to discuss playlist of musical selections for reception.

- ❑ Meet with photographer to discuss the ratio of candid to posed shots you want included in keepsake album and any specific photographs you want taken at reception and ceremony (pictures with grandma, the family dog Sparky, and so on).

- ❑ Bring fabric swatches to florist and finalize details for all wedding flowers.

- ❑ Call bridal shop to determine when gown will arrive. Shop for under-garments, hose, and jewelry. Make appointment for final fitting.

- ❑ Call caterer to determine what food and beverages you'll serve to the photographer, videographer, and band members.

- ❑ Make rehearsal arrangements. Remind every member of wedding party about rehearsal date, time, site.

- ❑ Arrange for wedding day transportation for important guests and bridal party.

❑ Make sure all official and civil documents are in order: baptismal, communion, or confirmation certificates, citizenship papers, proof of divorce, and so on.

❑ Order party favors to give to guests.

One Month Before

❑ Make appointment with hair and makeup stylists for bride and wedding party. Have a trial run with makeup artist to test for possible allergic reactions.

❑ Have final fitting for wedding gown.

❑ Have formal bridal portrait done.

❑ Submit wedding announcement (with black-and-white photo) to local newspaper.

❑ Begin moving into your new home.

❑ If taking your husband's name, make arrangements to change your name on Social Security card, driver's license, car registration and insurance, bank accounts, credit cards, insurance policies, school and office records, passport, voter registration.

❑ Draft a new will and change insurance beneficiary, if desired.

❑ Consult lawyer about prenuptial agreement, if desired.

❑ Fill out a change-of-address form at post office.

Two Weeks Before

- ❏ Go with fiancé to pick up marriage license.

- ❏ Address formal announcements so they can be mailed on the wedding day.

- ❏ Prepare seating chart for reception and rehearsal dinner.

- ❏ Assist out-of-town guests with baby-sitting arrangements.

- ❏ Prepare a wedding day flow-chart of events, hour by hour, to give to bridal party and all the key vendors: caterer, florist, photographer, officiant, band leader.

- ❏ Give caterer finalized guest count.

- ❏ Confirm honeymoon reservations and buy traveler's checks. Record the check numbers and amounts and leave a copy with someone at home who can be easily reached in case of emergency. Prepare a copy of your wedding itinerary for someone at home.

- ❏ Break in those wedding shoes! Wrap them in plastic or plastic bags and walk around the house!

One Week Before

- ❏ Pack for honeymoon. Be sure to include money, camera, passport, clothes, comfortable shoes, and medications.

- ❏ Give ushers instructions for seating guests at ceremony, with details about guests with special needs.

- ❑ Arrange for transportation from reception to airport, train, or hotel.

- ❑ Remind groom and groomsmen to pick up rental attire.

- ❑ Double-check that rental attire has all the right pieces: shoes, cummerbund, suspenders, belt, shirt, pants, tie, etc. and that *all the pieces fit.*

- ❑ Wrap gifts for attendants; present gifts at rehearsal dinner.

- ❑ Arrange for someone to collect gifts brought to reception and deliver them to your home.

- ❑ Confirm that airplane or train tickets are ticketed with correct date, time, and destination.

- ❑ Make final check with key players.

- ❑ Give best man a check for officiant's fee, to be delivered right after the ceremony.

- ❑ If desired, arrange for gift display. Checks may be displayed with the amount concealed. Display just one place setting of china, rather than the entire tableful.

- ❑ Arrange for transportation from the airport after the honeymoon.

- ❑ Arrange for someone to feed the family pet and pick up mail while you are away. Also, be sure someone will be watching your home during the wedding day.

- ❑ Confirm vocalist and organist.

- ❑ Arrange for backup transportation for bride and groom to ceremony, just in case.

- ❑ Make appointments for manicure and pedicure before wedding.

One Day Before

❏ Attend rehearsal and rehearsal dinner. Set a specific time for everyone in wedding party to meet on wedding day. Don't overindulge in
alcoholic drinks or caffeine.

❏ Determine where and when everyone will meet for wedding-day
photos.

❏ Place honeymoon luggage in car.

❏ Lay out all clothes, jewelry, and accessories for next day.

❏ Be sure wedding gown is stored away from heat, pets, water, very
young children, or an open window. (No kidding.)

❏ Arrange for maid of honor to bring "goodie bag" to reception
(see page 40).

❏ Discuss reception line procedure with parents and bridal party.

❏ If not using a professional consultant, assign someone else to run
interference for you on the wedding day. That way, the caterer or
florist know whom to ask questions.

❏ Get to bed early!

The Wedding Day

❏ Don't forget to eat something! It may be hours or all day until you have time for food, and many couples say they never even sit down for the reception meal.

❏ Have hair styled at least three to four hours before ceremony. If possible, relax and have a manicure.

❏ Allow one to two hours for leisurely dressing. Take care when applying makeup near the wedding gown! (If necessary, cover gown with smock or clean white sheet while applying makeup, or drape face with a soft cloth while slipping gown over head.)

❏ If taking pictures before the ceremony, bridal party should be *completely* ready and in place one to two hours before ceremony begins.

❏ The wedding music should start 30 to 45 minutes prior to ceremony.

❏ The groom's parents are seated a few minutes before ceremony begins, followed by the bride's parents.

❏ Be sure the best man and maid of honor sign the wedding certificate as witnesses.

❏ At the reception, it may be impossible to personally thank each guest for attending. In that case, the bride or groom toasts the guests and says a few words.

❏ Congratulations! Don't worry how the reception is going, just enjoy the day! Assign someone else to be in charge of last-minute snafus or instructions.

Ready-for-Anything Goodie Bag

A calm bride is a prepared bride. Avoid last-minute jitters and frantic searches by stocking necessaries in a zipped duffel bag or tote bag and arranging for the maid of honor or a bridesmaid to bring it to the ceremony and reception. The bag can double as a handy carry-on for honeymoon travel. Make sure it contains the following:

Scotch tape

Moist towelettes

Pad and pencil

Extra pantyhose (in shades for
    bride and bridesmaids)

Scissors

Safety pins

Hairpins

Hair spray

Brush and comb

Toothbrush and toothpaste

Mouthwash and breath mints

Camera with extra film,
    flashbulbs, batteries for
    candids

Comfortable shoe insoles

Antacid

Extension cord

Aspirin

Nail glue

Earring backs

Floral tape

Crackers

Extra floral pins (for boutonnieres)

Tissues

Stain remover

Contact lens solution

Extra pair of glasses

Paper cups

Nail polish and remover

Seltzer (it gets out some wine stains)

Extra maps and directions to ceremony/reception

Makeup and moisturizer

Medications

Loose change for vending machines

Extra pair of shoes to wear with gown (in case heel breaks or shoes get stained)

Needles and thread to match everyone's gowns

Extra pair of tights for flower girl

Krazy glue (great for reattaching beads and sequins)

Tampons

Baby powder (use it to camouflage wine or lipstick stains when posing for photographs)

Who Pays for What?

Every wedding is a personal celebration, and that means the players are free to decide how it will be bankrolled and who pays for what. But traditionally, the expenses are divvied up and borne by the bride, the groom, both sets of parents, and the attendants.

The Bride and Her Family

Wedding gown, veil, and accessories

Bridal consultant fee

Wedding cake

Flowers for bridesmaids, flower girl, ceremony, and reception

Luncheon for bridesmaids

Invitations, stationery, receptions cards, announcements

Engagement party costs

Reception: catering, music, linens, and rental items

Blood test for marriage license

Ceremony costs: organist, music, vocalist, site rental

Bride's trousseau

Photography

Bridal party transportation to ceremony and reception

Housing for out-of-town bridesmaids

Hotel room cost if bridal party will dress at a hotel

Music for reception and ceremony

A gift for the groom and groom's wedding ring (bride)

The Groom and His Family

Bride's engagement and wedding rings

Marriage license

Bride's bouquet

Corsages or flowers for mothers and grandmothers

Boutonnieres for ushers, ring bearers, and fathers

Housing for out-of-town ushers

Officiant's fee

Rehearsal dinner

Honeymoon

Groom's wedding outfit and clothing worn by his parents

Gift for the bride

Gifts for ushers

Transportation to honeymoon

Bridesmaids

Bridesmaid dress, shoes, and accessories

Travel to wedding town

Shower and wedding gifts to couple

Shower given by bridesmaids or maid of honor

Ushers

Travel expenses to wedding town

Wedding attire rental

Wedding gift to couple

Bachelor party given by best man or ushers

Bride and Groom

Gifts to attendants

Thank-you gifts to parents or those who helped with wedding

Anything else they wish to contribute

43

WEDDING BUDGET WORKSHEET

PRODUCT OR SERVICE	ESTIMATED EXPENSE	DEPOSIT PAID (DATE)	FINAL EXPENSE
Ceremony			
Officiant's fee			
Site fee			
Marriage license			
Ceremony music			
Vocalist			
Accessories (table runner, chalice, chuppah, candelabra, banners)			
Flowers			
Bridal bouquet			
Centerpieces			
Ceremony flowers			
Pew decorations			
Flowers for bride's home			
Bridesmaids' bouquets			
Corsages for mothers, grandmothers, honored guests, consultant			

44

Product or Service	Estimated Expense	Deposit Paid (date)	Final Expense
Flowers *continued*			
Boutonnieres			
Flower girl's basket, hair accessory, or wreath			
Rest-room centerpieces			
Flowers to decorate buffet (table and individual platters or serving dishes) and wedding cake			
Reception			
Catering			
Liquor			
Table linens			
Rental items (chairs, lighting, plants, chafing dishes, flatware)			
Music			
Parking			
Gratuities, taxes, and unusual fees like cake-cutting fee			
Cake, groom's cake, sweets table, or desserts			

45

Product or Service	Estimated Expense	Deposit Paid (date)	Final Expense
Reception *continued*			
Serving staff			
Site rental fee			
Party favors			
Champagne for toast			
Accessories (printed napkins, candles, matchbooks, place cards, candies)			
Attire			
Bride's gown			
Veil or headpiece			
Gloves			
Undergarments			
Accessories (garter, cloak or wrap, Bible to carry, etc.)			
Hose			
Shoes			
Alterations			
Jewelry			
Trousseau			
Groom's formal wear and accessories			

Product or Service	Estimated Expense	Deposit Paid (date)	Final Expense
Attire *continued*			
Bridesmaids' attire			
Groomsmen's attire			
Flower girl's/ring bearer's attire (usually bought by child's parents)			
Photography and Videography			
Keepsake album			
Engagement portrait			
Wedding portrait			
Extra prints			
Video			
Special effects			
Extra copies			
Personal camera, film, and batteries			
Music			
Reception			
Ceremony			
Rehearsal dinner music			

47

PRODUCT OR SERVICE	ESTIMATED EXPENSE	DEPOSIT PAID (DATE)	FINAL EXPENSE
Transportation			
Limousine			
Gondola or boat			
Horse and carriage			
Transportation to airport or honeymoon site			
Transportation for guests to out-of-the-way reception			
Honeymoon			
Accommodations			
Meals			
Train, plane, or automobile expenses			
Travel insurance			
Souvenirs			
Traveler's checks			
Prewedding parties			
Party invitations			
Engagement party			
Showers			

PRODUCT OR SERVICE	ESTIMATED EXPENSE	DEPOSIT PAID (DATE)	FINAL EXPENSE
Prewedding parties *continued*			
Rehearsal dinner			
Bachelor party			
Bridesmaids' luncheon			
Legal Fees			
Estate or tax planning			
Prenuptial agreement			
Will			
Rings			
Engagement			
Wedding			
Invitations and Stationery			
Invitations			
Place cards			
Response cards			
Announcements			
Personal stationery			

49

PRODUCT OR SERVICE	ESTIMATED EXPENSE	DEPOSIT PAID (DATE)	FINAL EXPENSE
Invitations and Stationery *continued*			
Thank-you notes			
Calligraphy			
Postage			
Wedding programs			
Maps and directions			
Miscellaneous			
Gifts for attendants			
Gifts for future spouse			
Telephone			
Fax fees			
Wedding insurance			
Telegrams			
Thank-you gifts to parents and anyone who helped with wedding			

15% Consultant

3% Invitations

2% Officiant

4% Miscellaneous

10% Music

10% Photography

Flowers 10%

Catering 46%

WHAT WILL IT COST US?

These vendor costs are based on a typical $15,000 wedding for 125 to 150 people, not including tax and gratuities.

Catering:	46%	$ 6,900	(dinner and beverages)
Consultant:	15%	$ 2,250	(for full-service wedding consultant)
Music:	10%	$ 1,500	(includes ceremony and reception, live band)
Invitations:	3%	$ 450	
Photography:	10%	$ 1,500	
Flowers:	10%	$ 1,500	
Miscellaneous:	4%	$ 600	
Officiant:	2%	$ 300	

(These figures will obviously vary according to couple and region of country)

Reprinted courtesy of Robbi Ernst III, from the June Wedding, Inc.,® An Association for Event Professionals, Wedding Consultant Training Manual, Fourth Edition.

WHO DOES WHAT?

Maid or Matron of Honor

A maid of honor is an unmarried woman; a matron of honor is married. Her main role is to help the bride with wedding planning. This might involve running errands, helping her select attire, addressing invitations, or making phone calls to vendors. Traditionally, she also hosts a shower or luncheon for the bride (or the couple). On the wedding day, she helps the bride get dressed, adjusts her veil and train before she starts down the aisle, holds her bouquet during the ceremony, and keeps the wedding ring until the ring exchange part of the ceremony.

She stands to the left of the groom in the receiving line and later sits to the left of the groom at the head table. Usually, a bride chooses a close friend or sister to be her honor attendant. But there have also been some cases where the bride's mother or stepmother is the matron of honor, or else a sister, friend, or relative of the groom. It's very important that the bride feels free to choose whomever *she* pleases, and not feel pressured by family politics. This is a once-in-a-lifetime decision.

The Best Man

Married or not, the groom's honor attendant is called the best man. He hosts or organizes a bachelor party for the groom, helps the groom dress for the wedding day, and signs the marriage license as an official witness. He also holds the officiant's fee until the groom needs it, and keeps the wedding ring until the groom needs it during the ceremony. The best man offers a toast to the couple at the reception, and he's the one responsible for arranging transportation or personally driving the bride and groom to their honeymoon hotel or to the airport. Often, the best man takes charge of collecting all the tuxedos for return to the rental shop.

The Bridesmaid(s)

There is only one maid/matron of honor, but there can be oodles of bridesmaids. Generally, a rule of thumb says you need one usher for every fifty guests, and sometimes people translate that to also mean one bridesmaid for every usher. But if the bride wants six bridesmaids and the groom wants two ushers, so be it. Bridesmaids assist the honor attendant with planning a shower or luncheon for the bride. They take part in all the prewedding celebrations and walk behind the ushers during the processional. In the receiving line, they stand to the left of the maid of honor. At the wedding, their main job is to sit at the head table and urge all the single women to join in the bouquet-tossing ritual.

The Usher(s)

In addition to helping the groom on his wedding day, ushers serve an important purpose: They seat guests as they arrive at the ceremony. If the guest is female, the usher offers his right arm. If the guest is male, the usher walks along his left side. Guests of the bride are seated on the left side of the church, synagogue, or ceremony room; guests of the groom are seated on the right. Just before the bride walks down the aisle, two ushers escort the mother of the groom to her seat; then they escort the mother of the bride to her seat. This signals the beginning of the ceremony! Sometimes the ushers roll out a red or white carpet for the bride to tread upon down the aisle. Following the ceremony, the ushers have the task of helping elderly or special-needs guests to their cars. They also do a quick check of the sanctuary or room to make sure no one left anything behind.

Handy Tip:

Not sure what to do, where to stand, or when to do it? Wedding Solutions, a professional wedding planning company based in San Diego, California, has published a handy little booklet of tear-out cards called *Wedding Party Responsibility Cards* (1995; $6.95, paperback). The cards fold conveniently to fit into a purse or pocket and list the traditional responsibilities of each member of the wedding party (including both sets of parents), where they stand during the ceremony processional and recessional, and what their financial responsibilities typically include.

Chapter Three

The Wedding Consultant

Wedding planning can be practically worry-free with the help of
a professional consultant, especially when you don't have the time—
or the expertise—to plan such an important celebration on your own.

Forget the movie industry image of the pompous bridal consultant who brow-beats clients into staging an expensive extravaganza. While wedding consultants were once hired primarily by the rich and famous, consultants today are engaged by anyone who simply needs an extra set of hands and knowledge of local vendors to create magic from any budget.

Most engaged couples today can use that extra help. The bride is often working, and so is her mother, who traditionally helped with wedding planning. On top of it all, the couple may be living or working in one city while trying to plan a wedding in another.

How do you find a clergyman or a specialty orchid grower in Tallahassee when you're living in Toledo? Professional consultants will have those resources at their fingertips, and are also highly skilled in the mechanics of party planning: choosing vendors, negotiating contracts, locating the perfect antique lace veil or table linens, booking a reception site, or flying in tropical flowers in the exact shade of yellow the bride fancies.

Ideally, a consultant can save you time, worry, and stress and help you avoid making costly mistakes. ("You mean we don't need three pounds of Beluga caviar per person?")

A wedding consultant usually specializes in the planning or coordination of the wedding. Some also have experience planning corporate or special events for the business community and charity balls (a real plus if yours will be a themed reception or staged in an unusual setting). Many have degrees in business or are highly skilled in the financial aspects of wedding planning.

"You use a professional to prepare your taxes, maintain your car, or fix your plumbing," notes Gerard Monaghan, president of the Association of Bridal Consultants (A.B.C.) in New Milford, Connecticut. "Why not let a professional help you plan this important day?"

While many wedding consultants work independently, others are affiliated with a bridal shop, hotel, retail shop, or any other wedding-related business.

WHERE DID YOU LEARN TO DO THIS?

Since vendors of all stripe (and level of skill) are often generically listed in the yellow pages as wedding consultants, it's very important to ask about specific training and professional credentials. What kind of certification program has he or she completed? Where? When? Does he or she maintain his or her credentials through continuing education and experience in the field?

The advantage of a professional consultant is that you can pay for only those wedding services you want and need. That means you needn't feel obliged to let someone else run the show. Consultants may be hired on an hourly or project basis, for anywhere from one or three initial planning sessions to coordinating the entire wedding, from engagement party through to honeymoon itinerary.

Services might include designing a wedding theme, interviewing and hiring vendors, negotiating prices, answering questions about etiquette, scheduling appointments, or designing a wedding-day flow chart. Or it could mean just engaging a professional to stand by at the ceremony to fluff dresses (and calm nerves!) and make sure everything runs smoothly.

"The consultant's role is to bring the bride's wishes to fruition, beginning with helping her define a budget," says professional consultant Beverly Dembo of Dembo Productions in Chicago. "The idea is that a good consultant will know resources at different price ranges, and people who have proven themselves to be consistently dependable and outstanding in their fields."

Don't underestimate the power of this knowledge and experience. Imagine how much time and money you can save if someone else already has the scoop

57

on which harpists can be trusted to play beautifully and which caterers have access to linens in every color imaginable.

Planning many weddings each year gives consultants the inside track on which local vendors are the cream of the crop, notes master bridal consultant Teddy Lenderman of Terre Haute, Indiana, author of *The Complete Idiot's Guide to the Perfect Wedding*. She says of the thirty photographers typically listed in the local phone book, a consultant can tell you which are the top five or six in any price range. "I *know* all that information," she says. "The average person planning a wedding doesn't have a clue."

Nationwide, fees vary widely from region to region and according to the size and complexity of the wedding. A consultant may charge an hourly or flat rate, or a percentage of the total wedding budget.

Generally, fees range anywhere from 5 to 15 percent of the total wedding costs. Hourly rates can be anywhere from $25 for vendor referrals to $75 to $300 for a series of initial consultations. Comprehensive wedding planning services can cost several thousand dollars. Again, these figures are all relative, since costs can be considerably higher in major cities and vary with wedding size and services included.

"Our belief is that much of the planning should be accomplished through a great deal of communication with the bride and all of the wedding professionals long before the actual day," says Lyn Rosenfield, co-owner with Gaye Greenamyer of Green Rose Wedding Coordinators in Carrollton, Texas. "Even the ring bearer should know what will transpire on that special day and know what his duties are."

How to Find a Consultant

Ask for referrals from friends. Caterers, florists, and photographers also work hand in hand with consultants and may be a source of honest, reliable information. Try calling the catering director at several of the best hotels in town or the heads of several local bridal shops, and ask them for recommendations. Does the local college or adult education division offer a course in wedding planning? Ask the instructor for referrals. And of course newlyweds who have recently used a consultant are a fountain of information.

Nationwide, there are several major associations devoted to training and certifying bridal consultants. All will provide referrals to consultants in your area.

- ❀ June Wedding, Inc.®
  An Association for Event Professionals
  8514 FM 3117
  Temple, Texas 76501-7206
  (817)983-3596
  Email:junewed@wm.com;URL;http://www.dpatch.com/JWI.
  June Wedding, Inc., also provides referrals to special-event professionals for corporate and private parties.

- ❀ The Association of Bridal Consultants (A.B.C.)
  200 Chestnutland Rd.
  New Milford, CT 06776-2521
  (203) 355-0464

- ❀ National Bridal Service (N.B.S.)
  3122 West Cary St.
  Richmond, VA 23221
  (804) 355-6945

- ❀ The Association of Certified Professional
  Wedding Consultants
  7791 Prestwick Circle
  San Jose, CA 95135
  (408) 223-5686

THINGS TO KEEP IN MIND

Some experts say be wary of the consultant who receives a commission from vendor referrals, since that might limit the consultant's resources, which is not always in the best interest of the client. Others argue that a reputable consultant will recommend only vendors who offer superior service and value to clients.

Another sticky issue is payment by percentage. Some consultants charge a percentage of the total wedding budget. An unscrupulous consultant may thus not be as motivated to negotiate for lower prices for the couple if he is getting a percentage of the final tab. An ethical consultant, however, will work to provide the highest quality at the lowest cost. How will you know the difference? Hopefully, you can trust the person or vendor who recommended the consultant in the first place. You can also be up front and ask the consultant how she charges. If she dances around the percentage issue or tells you it's none of your business what commissions she receives from other vendors, think twice about hiring her. Remember, the consultant's reputation—and future business—depends on the quality of the services you receive and the vendors he hires on your behalf.

If the consultant charges by a percentage, make sure that it's specified at the initial meeting and put in the contract. The percentage issue can pose a problem, since a wedding often ends up costing more than anticipated by most couples inexperienced in planning a big party.

Robbi Ernst of June Wedding, Inc.,® in Temple, Texas advises couples to ascertain a professional's training and whether he or she has a business license. These details are paramount, says Ernst, whose international association offers a comprehensive training and certification program and even requires its member to have appropriate health and insurance permits.

While a consultant can help you negotiate the details of all contracts with vendors, couples should still sign those contracts themselves, rather than letting the consultant do it on their behalf. That way, payment is made directly to the vendor, and the newlyweds have more recourse if there is a problem later.

"It's never too early to start planning. We ask a lot of questions early on. Do you want the bouquet on the cake table? Who will be responsible for the guest book? Where do you want to display it? Who is bringing the flowers from the church to the reception site? Who is riding to the wedding with whom? Who is responsible for the cake top? For the gown when you leave the reception? Does the gown go to an heirloomer? What is the address? All this advance planning relieves a lot of stress!"

—Lyn Rosenfield and Gaye Greenamyer, co-owners of
Green Rose Wedding Coordinators, Carrollton, Texas

MAKING WEDDING DREAMS COME TRUE

Consultants are called upon to do everything from the mundane to the magical.

They have been known to help brides remove last-minute lipstick stains from their gowns, calm jittery mothers of the bride, and arrange for hot-air balloons to whisk a couple away from their reception. They have also been called upon to create themed receptions that make for unforgettable events and

61

arrange for party favors, like baseball-shaped cookies, that reflect the couple's personalities or interests.

For a couple who had used a tarot card reader to predict their wedding date, Ernst orchestrated a gypsy-themed wedding, complete with strolling violinists, linen tablecloths decorated with stars, and real psychics and tarot card readers to provide entertainment. Party favors included chocolate moons and stars in pretty boxes, and every guest got a decorative mask to wear while dancing. "It wasn't an expensive theme," Ernst says. "And the bride and groom were so excited because they got thank-you notes from their guests!"

Consultant Patticia Bruneau of L'Affaire Du Temps worked on an ocean-themed wedding where the reception was held on a beach. The centerpieces were glass bowls with goldfish swimming in them, and everything had seashells on it. "We put sand on the tables," she recalls. "At the end of the reception, all the children took a goldfish home!"

For a holiday wedding, Bruneau arranged for a calligrapher to write the couple's names on clear glass Christmas ornaments, which provided festive decoration and were used as party favors.

Sometimes consultants dabble in crisis management. The most bizarre request ever received by consultant Denise Winkelstein of Accents: Wedding and Event Planning in San Mateo, California, was to "create a minister in a hurry." The bride wanted her college youth minister to officiate at her wedding, but when his official status had still not come through just days before the ceremony, Winkelstein helped him obtain civil officiant status for the day. "This involved contacting the local county clerk and completing forms or being interviewed by the clerk. They then granted deputy commissioner of marriage status for one day," she explained. "Anyone can do this. We had another couple who had the bride's brother—an engineer by trade—perform the ceremony they wrote together."

Michelle Hodges, of I Do Weddings and Events in San Jose, California, once filled an unusual request for an Elvis Presley impersonator for a couple's reception and a mariachi band for their rehearsal dinner. She has also arranged for a couple to exchange vows on the steps of a Chinese water temple, where the couple's first toast was with water instead of champagne, to symbolize purity.

Hodges often works with brides planning long-distance weddings. To one in particular, who was overwhelmed at moving across the country from Pennsylvania to California and planning a formal wedding at the same time, Hodges suggested making a collage from magazine clippings. Then she corresponded with the couple by phone and fax and arranged every single detail for them. When the couple arrived in California one week before the wedding, they were given a complete itinerary to follow, which included a romantic afternoon alone in San Francisco.

WHAT TO ASK WHEN HIRING A WEDDING CONSULTANT

- ❁ How do you charge? Flat fee? Percentage of total wedding budget? By the hour? By the contracted meeting?
- ❁ How will you be paid? (installments? retainer?)
- ❁ How long have you been in business, and what kind of professional training or certification have you received? (Not all states require a business license, but if your state does, it should be prominently displayed.)

63

- ❀ If need be, can you work entirely by phone and fax with a couple, or just meet them for an initial session or on the day of the wedding? (This is possible, but it's *always* a better idea to meet personally at least once or twice.)

- ❀ How many weddings have you worked on?

- ❀ What is the full range of services you offer?

- ❀ What is your specialty? (Some consultants are whizzes at planning long-distance weddings or staging weddings in unusual settings like a winery or historic mansion.)

- ❀ What is the average budget for the weddings you work on?

- ❀ What kind of health permits, insurance, and liability coverage do you have?

- ❀ What kind of training or certification have you completed?

- ❀ What do you include in a contract? (Be sure it lists all fees, specific services to be provided, and deadlines to be met.)

- ❀ Do you prepare a wedding-day schedule of events?

- ❀ How will you keep us informed of which tasks have been accomplished and when?

- ❀ How do you view your role?

- ❀ How will you be attired on the wedding day?

- ❀ Do you work on more than one wedding in a day? (This can be a potential problem if the consultant must dash from your wedding to another one.)

THE WEDDING CONSULTANT WEARS MANY HATS

A trained consultant usually takes on all these roles:

Efficiency expert and organizer

Advocate, to get you the best services, quality and prices

Coordinator, to assure that the florist and caterer collaborate on cake decorations

Supervisor, to oversee all the work by the vendors you've engaged

Scheduler, to anticipate problems and tell everyone what to do and when

Extra set of hands, to handle the details

Mediator, to run interference with vendors and family members

Financial planner, to work within a budget and help you understand costs and services

Creative director, with the expertise and vision to create a special theme or look

Legal expert, skilled in the mechanics of contracts and payments

Diplomat, to sweetly explain to a difficult cousin why toddlers have not been invited

Advance man, to travel cross-country or across town to handle your arrangements

Industry expert, savvy about the latest wedding trends

Independent third party, for solving problems outside family embroilments

Why not just plan the wedding yourself? Well, you can! Planning the wedding is certainly part of the joy of preparing for marriage. But sometimes couples just don't have the time, the money, or the interest to do it themselves and want to be spared the hassle.

Why not just ask a friend or relative to do it for you? Think long and hard about this. While someone close to you may know your tastes and have a sincere interest in your happiness, remember that weddings are often the arena for all kinds of emotional blowouts.

Planning a wedding is a serious investment of time and money, and problems and "family situations" invariably crop up. Do you want someone emotionally connected to you to be making the big decisions and giving you honest opinions ("That wedding dress does *nothing* for you"), or would you benefit from someone neutral, with the skill and expertise to step back and make impartial decisions?

Also, asking a loved one to do the major legwork means she or he may miss out on being a guest and enjoying the wedding. If hiring a consultant is out of the question, consider assigning single, specific tasks to loved ones. But be sure that a detached third party is there on the wedding day to help out in case a button pops off or the flowers show up at the wrong place. The couple, their parents, and the bridal party will invariably be too preoccupied to drop everything and start problem solving ten minutes before going down the aisle.

Chapter Four

The Bridal Gift Registry

The first bridal registry probably came about
after one too many brides got one too many toasters.

It's not unusual for engaged couples to receive duplicate gifts during the rounds of prewedding parties and showers. That can mean four steam irons, too many teacups, and enough crystal goblets for a White House state dinner.

To avoid the problem of duplications and provide a convenience for guests, think carefully about what you'll need for your new home and register these choices through a bridal registry. Registering simply means recording your preferences (and quantities) in a variety of categories, along with the wedding date, color and pattern choices, and where the gifts may be sent. The store registry keeps this information on file for guests to consult. As a result, the couple receives gifts they love and can really use, and most guests appreciate not having to guess about their wish list.

This free service was once limited to department stores with large table-setting departments. Nowadays, however, bride and groom can register at specialty emporiums, bed-and-bath shops, clothing stores, discount retailers, bookstores, through mail-order catalogues, and at home-improvement centers and sporting-goods stores. Some couples have even "registered" for wedding gifts in the form of donations to their favorite charity, college alumni fund, or scholarship endowment.

How does a registry work? Guests simply visit the store's local branch or ask for the couple's "wish list" by fax, mail, or phone. Stores with computerized registries can supply the information nationwide at the touch of a button. As gifts are purchased, they're removed from the list.

Most of the Target stores throughout the country, for instance, now offer a computerized bridal registry called Club Wedd. Target, a division of Dayton Hudson Corporation, is a Minneapolis-based quality discount retailer. Engaged couples enter basic information about their wedding into a computer kiosk at any branch. Then they receive a hand-held bar-code scanner "gun" to register choices around the store, which are automatically recorded in a computer.

This high-tech registry service is similar to those at many different kinds of stores nationwide. Some simply have free-standing computer kiosks or booths set up where the future newlyweds register choices on the spot.

GOBLETS, GRILLS, OR GUTTERS?

Recognizing that today's couples are marrying later and may not need dinner plates or towels, many home-improvement stores have set up registry services for household items modern couples say they *really* need—like paint, lumber, cabinets, automobile tires, or rain gutters.

Based in Atlanta, the Home Depot chain of home-improvement centers offers a computerized bridal registry service in all of its 334 stores, in twenty-eight states. A bridal consultant is available in each store to personally escort the couple up and down the aisles and record their choices.

"We have noticed people register for everything you can imagine—from a doorbell for their new home to shrubs for their new lawn!" says company spokeswoman Jenifer Swearingen. Guests can then go in as a group and buy, say, a gas grill.

It's never too early or late to register. Some brides do it as soon as the engagement is announced, since friends and relatives will appreciate ideas for engagement and shower gifts.

Longing for a canoe? A good destination might be the gift registry service offered by L.L. Bean, the outdoor sporting specialties retail store and mail-order operation based in Freeport, Maine. Couples often register there for home furnishings like sheets, couches, tables, or big-ticket sporting goods like canoes and backpacks.

69

Many gift registries keep the selections on file for at least a year, a boon to wedding guests who often call back after the wedding and ask for suggestions for holiday and birthday gifts for the newlyweds!

Let loved ones know where you are registered. Etiquette experts say it's fine to include where the bride is registered on a shower invitation, but *never* appropriate for a wedding invitation.

Most stores offering a gift registry also provide the services of a bridal consultant to help a couple define their tastes and develop preferences based on lifestyle and entertaining requirements. This is a useful free service. Most engaged couples have a fairly good idea of whether they are more likely to host formal dinners for twenty on a regular basis or invite a small circle of friends over for take-out food. But it's not as easy to determine just how many berry spoons or place settings your shared lifestyle will require. The consultant can help mix and match china patterns and flatware, answer questions about decorating schemes, and generally help pull it all together.

Are you combining two homes or starting from scratch? Will you do a lot of formal entertaining as a married couple? What kind of decorating scheme do you both favor? Popular styles include traditional, contemporary, southwestern, colonial, and country. Do you have space or storage limitations? Budget considerations? What colors do you both prefer?

A registry consultant can help you answer these questions and recommend items that complement pieces you already have. A consultant can also tell you about upcoming store product demonstrations, fashion shows, or sales.

MAKING CHOICES AS A COUPLE

Most brides register with their future husbands. It's a great way to plan your future together while learning to negotiate and develop respect for each other's tastes.

The thoughtful bride and groom will register gift selections in a wide range of prices, which gives guests more flexibility in making choices. It's okay to register selections at more than one store, but avoid overlapping items at both places, or you may defeat your purpose.

A bridal registry can work for you even after the wedding. If you didn't receive all the items you registered as gifts, many bridal registries offer special discounts or bonus gifts if you decide to buy them for yourself.

"We turned our reception into a double celebration. My wife was scheduled to receive her master's degree at the same time our ceremony was slated to begin. Her parents were determined that she get her diploma, so they clandestinely had the university mail her diploma to them. You should have seen Susan's face when we handed her the degree just after the best man and maid of honor delivered their toasts. As an official at the university so aptly put it, she earned her MRS. and MBA in the same day."

—Scott L. Smith, a Connecticut May bridegroom

WEDDING REGISTRY CHECKLIST

What do we really *need*, and what would we really *love* to have?

Asking yourselves these questions can make registering for gifts much easier, and the answers will tell you a lot about your planned lifestyle together. (After all, why feel pressured to register for fine crystal and china if you don't really think you'll use them?)

A good place to begin is by prioritizing these general categories:

- Formal dinnerware
- Silver or silverplate flatware
- Fine crystal
- Serving accessories
- Home furnishings
- Table linens
- Decorative accessories
- Hobby and sporting goods
- Kitchen accessories and gadgets
- Casual dinnerware
- Stainless flatware
- Glasses and barware
- Cookware/bakeware
- Personal care products
- Bed and bath items
- Patio and garden items
- Hardware and tools

Sample Registry Checklist

Every store has its own special registry list, so the following is a general guideline. Remember, as a convenience to you and your guests, most stores will also allow you to write in items they don't carry.

If a store you favor does not have a registry, ask to establish one or at least keep a list of your preferences on hand. Most bridal magazines publish a registry checklist in each issue. Fill one out and bring it with you for ease in making selections.

Formal Dinnerware/Casual Dinnerware

List the manufacturer, pattern name, and quantity

Place settings
Salad/dessert plates
Soup bowls
Coffee server
Soup plates
Serving bowls
Dinner plates

Teacups and saucers
Fruit bowls
Teapot
Platters
Gravy boat
Covered vegetable
   and casserole dishes

Flatware: stainless and/or silver (or silverplate)

List the manufacturer, pattern name, and quantity

Place knives, forks, and spoons
Creamed-soupspoons
Butter serving knife
Berry spoon/pierced teaspoon
Well-and-tree platter
Additional serving pieces
   (spaghetti tongs, salad tongs,
   serving spoons, cheese knife)

Soup spoons
Butter spreaders
Cold meat fork
Gravy ladle
Pie/cake server
Sugar spoon
Silver chest
Candlesticks

73

Glasses and Barware

Water goblets
Highball glasses
On-the-rocks glasses
Old-fashioned glasses
Ice bucket and tongs
Wine rack
Bar utensils
Portable drinks cooler
Iced tea or
   cold beverage glasses (12 oz.)

Wineglasses (all purpose)
Shot glasses
Beer/pilsner glasses
Decanter
Cocktail shaker
Vacuum seal caps
Pitcher
Coasters
Cocktail napkins
Juice glasses

Serving Accessories

Platters

Covered casserole dishes

Compote dish

Trivets

Trays

Bread basket

Bowls

Chafing dish

Nut dish

Cutting board

Extra serving spoons

Covered cake plate

Salad bowl/tongs or
serving utensils

Fine Crystal

Tumblers

Red wine

Champagne glasses
(flute, tulip, or sherbet shaped)

Brandy snifter

White wine

Cordial/liqueur glasses

Linens and Bedroom Items

Fitted and flat sheets

Mattress pad

Comforter

Matching curtains or valances

Blankets/quilts/
duvet/duvet covers

Pillows, shams, and pillowcases

Dust ruffle (bedskirt)

Bedspread

Patchwork quilt

Lightweight thermal blanket

Towels

Table Linens

Place mats

Tablecloths (size and shape:
round, square, rectangle, oval)

Napkins

Napkin rings

Runners

Bath Linens and Accessories

Bath towels

Hand towels

Washcloths

Guest towels

Bath mat and bath sheet

Shower curtain
(and rings and curtain liner)

Scale

Hamper

Bathroom rug

Bathroom curtains

Accessories: soap dish,
toothbrush holder, towel rack,
tissue-box cover, wastebasket

Kitchen Items

Canisters

Spice rack

Coffee grinder

Storage containers

Utensils and gadgets

Cookbooks

Cookie jar

Knife storage block

Trivets and coasters

Cookware (skillet, fry pan,
saucepans, large soup pot,
tea kettle)

Blender

Dishcloths and towels

Oven mitt and pot holders

Crockpot or slow cooker

Mixing bowl set

Coffeemaker

Rack for hanging pots or utensils

Timer

Kitchen mixer

Bakeware (baking pans,
cookie sheets, loaf pan,
Bundt pan, tube pan)

Home Furnishings

Rugs

Curtains

Cedar chest

Tray tables

Chairs

Clock

Mirrors

Paintings or decorative art

Fireplace set

Fans

Lamps

Home Electrics and Electronics

Stereo equipment

Videocassette recorder

Smoke detector

Iron/ironing board

Breadmaker

Cappuccino/espresso maker

Pasta maker

Vacuum cleaner

Flashlights

Fire extinguisher

Home canning equipment
(steam bath pot, jars,
tongs, rings, and lids)

Phone

Television

Answering machine

Fax machine

Food processor

Electric can opener

Popcorn maker

Blender/mixer

Electric broom

Toaster

Toaster oven

Sewing machine

Microwave oven or convection oven

Other Items to Consider

Garden and patio furnishings

Hardware and tools

Luggage

Sporting equipment

Exercise equipment

Bookcases

Garage accessories
(extension cords, ladder,
paint, tools, saw, sawhorse,
metal storage cabinets)

Power tools

Paint or lumber for home projects

Picnic table and benches

Outdoor grill

Camera

VCR

Camcorder

Trellis or arbor

Trees, seedlings, and outdoor
plantings

Chapter Five

Wedding Parties and Showers

Now that you are engaged, get ready for a heady whirl of
parties and celebrations leading up to the wedding!

This is the fun part of wedding festivities, and couples are often surprised to learn just how many people want to help them celebrate their joy and good fortune. Beginning with the engagement party and ending with the walk down the aisle, a couple may become guests of honor at showers or a bachelor/bachelorette party and also play host at other parties to thank their family and friends.

WEDDING SHOWERS: YOURS, MINE, AND OURS

Legend has it that the first bridal shower was given for a Dutch bride with a broken heart.

Her father had refused to give her a dowry because she intended to marry a poor miller. The lovers married despite the threat of poverty, and the groom's friends pitched in and "showered" the bride with gifts of household necessities for their new home. Thanks to the shower, the bride's heart was mended—and her cupboard was stocked.

That generous practice has become a wedding tradition, occasionally snowballing into multiple showers given by friends, bridesmaids, business associates, and both families. But this "more is better" trend has also generated some controversy. Advice columnist Ann Landers notes wedding showers can cause ill will when guests are expected to show up at several of them—toting, naturally, a gift each time. I once came across a New York City bride who had been given eight showers! Her wedding guest list topped more than four hundred and people kept throwing showers for her left and right. Attending them became something of a part-time job for her, and probably a trial for those who wound up on several guest lists!

A thoughtful hostess will inquire whether anyone else is having a shower for the bride and resist inviting guests to more than one. She will also ask the bride what she wants and needs and whether she has color preferences.

SHOWERS OVER THE YEARS

Bridal showers were once primarily household-stocking parties and became the only place where a young woman could be assured of getting more canisters, fish forks, and cheese graters than she'd use in a lifetime.

In early America, showers were a small, cozy party where women got together to toast the bride-to-be and help her sew a wedding quilt to be used in her home. It was an important rite of passage and a signal to the community that the young woman was assuming a new role in society.

Contemporary "kitchen" showers were the standard in recent decades, wherein guests often arrived with the nuts and bolts—linens, flatware, pots and pans, gadgets, coffee makers, juice glasses—that make a house a home. While the bride and her female friends opened gifts and sipped pink punch, the groom was expected to stay away until it was time to ogle the gifts and load them into the car.

More recently, showers have evolved into "lifestyle" parties, since today's bride and groom often come to the marriage with households firmly established. Thus, specialty showers with themes chosen to meet the needs of the specific couple are a trend. And many showers are now co-ed affairs, or even "groom showers," where guests arrive with gifts for recreation or hobbies, as well as furnishings, fine wines, camping gear, or power tools.

One Connecticut bride was thrown a surprise Victorian tea-party shower in the conservatory of a local museum. Guests gathered to sip tea in china cups and nibble cookies, tea sandwiches, and trifle made from recipes from Buckingham Palace and the Savoy Hotel in London. The wedding party

79

dressed in long skirts, romantic hats, and upswirled hairdos, and each center-piece was fashioned from an antique teapot. (The groom's mother had spent a year hunting down special teapots at estate sales.) Each guest took home an antique cup and saucer as a party favor.

Surprise showers make for lots of hoopla and high drama, but it may be necessary to plan the event with the bride if she travels a great deal or has an unpredictable schedule. If the shower is a surprise, be sure the ruse to get the bride there includes notifying her of proper attire. (Pity the poor bride antici-pating a picnic who is thrust into a swanky restaurant in jeans and T-shirt!)

Generally, it's thoughtful to include only those guests who are also invited to the wedding, unless it's an office shower hosted by co-workers who don't expect a wedding invitation but want to fete the bride.

Who hosts a bridal shower? Although bridal attendants are not technically obligated to give the bride a shower, most traditionally do so. Showers are also given by friends, the honor attendant, the best man, or business associates.

Etiquette experts are divided on the issue of whether close family members should host. Some insist a shower should never be hosted by the bride or groom's mother or immediate family. Others say this bit of protocol is out-dated. Showers held at restaurants or catering halls with many guests have become popular—and costly—and it's not unusual to find, say, the mother of the bride offering to help pay the expenses.

No matter who plays host, the bride should *never* be asked to contribute to shower expenses.

Showers are generally held two to six weeks before the wedding, but there's no hard-and-fast rule. If the bride lives out of town, it may be necessary to schedule the party for when she is on hand for a dress fitting, or in the final days before the wedding. (Likewise, if most of the guests will be in town briefly for the wedding, it may be necessary to squeeze in the party just prior to the wedding.)

Unlike an engagement party, the gifts at a shower are always opened in the presence of everyone. To make thank-you writing easier, ask a friend to record the gifts and givers. If there are many guests and dozens of gifts to open, the bridesmaids may be called upon to unwrap the gifts and present them with the enclosure card to the bride.

Shower games such as charades or Pop the Question (where each guest asks the bride a question about love or romance as she opens her gift) may be played, and it's traditional for the ribbons and bows from each gift to be made into a bouquet or bonnet for the bride to carry or wear at the wedding rehearsal.

POPULAR SHOWER THEMES

Round-the-Clock Shower On the invitation, guests are assigned an hour of the day (say, 7:00 A.M.) and challenged to bring a gift appropriate to that hour (an alarm clock or coffeemaker, for instance).

Kitchen Shower All the household staples are welcome—gadgets, dish towels, spice rack, canisters, trivets, cookware. Party favors might include a beribboned wooden spoon or refrigerator magnets.

Entertainment Shower Guests bring gifts for hobbies and entertainment, including theater, movie, or sports tickets; videos, or sporting equipment. Or guests can pool their resources for a big gift like a television, camcorder, or outdoor grill.

Gourmet Shower Do the bride and groom love to cook and entertain? Gather for a fabulous special meal and bring gift certificates for fine dining, cookbooks, a subscription to a cooking magazine, kitchen gadgets, china, glassware, cappuccino maker, or gift certificate for a cooking course.

Handyman Shower Get ready to work! At this service shower bring a hammer, nails, buckets of paint, and whatever is needed to spruce up the couple's house or apartment. Gifts might include tools, materials, a gift certificate to a hardware store, or the services of a professional painter, plumber, electrician, or craftsman.

Bar Shower Here's the chance to stock the couple's bar with glassware, tongs, ice bucket, corkscrew, napkins with silly messages, wine rack, fine wines, or boutique beers.

Thanks-for-the-Memories Shower A fun party for close friends and family of the bride. Everyone is asked to bring old photographs of the bride from her childhood or teenage years and to write a poem or letter to her recalling the happy times they've spent together and good wishes for the future. As each guest shares a memory, the letters and photographs are placed in an heirloom scrapbook for the bride to keep.

Lingerie Shower Pajamas, nightgowns, slippers, down pillows, bed linens, a robe, bath bubbles, fragrances, slips, teddies, or any kind of lingerie.

Holiday Shower Homemade Christmas decorations and holiday stockings; red, white, and blue linens and glassware or barbecue utensils for the Fourth of July; decorated papier-mâché eggs and moss-covered wreaths for Easter; confetti, candles, and paper hats for New Year's Eve. The bride will end up with a year's worth of household decorations.

THE BRIDESMAIDS' PARTY

Think about it: Your maid of honor and attendants have probably managed details throughout the wedding planning to help you cope and prepare. Here's a chance to honor them in return.

Traditionally, the bridesmaids' party was a luncheon held on the day of the wedding. These days, the celebration is typically held within a week or two of the wedding, since the final days before the wedding are chockablock with activities. The party may be a breakfast, luncheon, afternoon tea, or dinner held in a private home, club, or restaurant. Spas and upscale hair salons are becoming popular venues for the bridesmaids' luncheon, and they often sponsor a special "Wedding Day of Beauty" party package to pamper the bride and her attendants with hairstyling and makeup sessions, manicures or massage. Generally, only the female attendants, flower girl, bride's mother and sisters, and groom's mother and sisters are present. But this can also be a good time to include out-of-town guests.

The bride is usually the hostess, since the purpose of the party is for her to say thank you to her attendants, but the bridesmaids' party may also be hosted and organized by a close friend or female relative. This is the time for the bride to say a few words of sincere thanks and to present her attendants with small, personal gifts. Monogrammed notepaper, a necklace, silver picture frame, or engraved bracelet are welcome choices.

In the southern regions of America, it's a custom at the bridesmaids' party for the cake (traditionally pink) to contain good-luck charms. These small charms, which may be baked into the cake or attached to ribbons inserted between the layers, may include a coin (for riches), a horseshoe or wishbone (for luck), a ring (for marriage), or a heart (for love). Each bridesmaid pulls a ribbon that supposedly carries with it the riches its charm symbolizes.

Sticky Situations:

What if I have never met many of the guests at my shower before and don't even know who to thank for gifts?

Once intimate parties for close family and friends, showers are now often extravaganzas that include every single female wedding guest. If you don't know all the guests, be sure to ask someone who does to sit beside you. This attendant might open the card while you are unwrapping the gift and announce the name of the giver, while discreetly nodding her head or signaling where the person is sitting.

Or you can take the direct approach and begin the gift opening with the announcement, "I haven't had the pleasure of meeting you in person yet. I would love to thank everyone personally for coming here to share my joy, so would you kindly introduce yourselves to me as we go along?"

THE BACHELOR PARTY

Typically hosted by the best man or bridegroom's close friends, the bachelor party is generally a males-only event that toasts the bridegroom's final days of "freedom" and brings together his best buddies for the last hurrah to bachelorhood.

According to one wedding legend, the original purpose of a bachelor party was to raise funds for the bridegroom so that he could afford to go drinking with his friends after marriage—when the wife took control of all finances. Other wedding historians say the bachelor party is a symbolic farewell to sexual freedom and a ritual that formally announces the bride-groom's impending monogamy.

Brides are often anxious about sending their bridegrooms off to a bachelor party because they've heard the ritual is associated with "temptation" and have listened to horror stories about wild drinking, gambling, or partying with strippers or prostitutes.

The truth is, most bachelor parties are relatively tame affairs. The event is often a time for old friends to gather, reminisce, and wish the bridegroom well. Some parties include visits to bars or burlesque shows and viewing of adult movies; others might include a dinner in a nice restaurant, a men's-night-out poker game, or tailgate party and tickets to a ball game. The words *bachelor party* need not translate to "night of debauchery."

It's important for the party organizers to keep the bridegroom's feelings and personality in mind when planning the venue and activities. I've known bridegrooms who were mortified at the kind of wild antics their friends planned for them and felt ungrateful and miserable at the same time.

Traditionally, the bachelor party is held the night before the wedding. Since this often conflicts with the rehearsal dinner (and the bridegroom ends up bleary-eyed at the ceremony), it's usual for the men to get together a week or several days before the wedding to allow time to recuperate. And brides-maids are often opting to forgo a quiet tea party for a bachelorette bash and night on the town featuring dinner, theater, or a visit to a nightclub.

Still nervous about what might go on at the bachelor party? Make a point of discussing your fears and concerns openly with your fiancé. This isn't the time to leave "trust" issues unresolved.

85

THE REHEARSAL DINNER

Some sort of party is always held immediately following the wedding rehearsal, on the day before the big event. Originally held to make enough racket to scare away evil spirits, the rehearsal dinner is a time for the couple, immediate families, attendants/ushers and their spouses, clergyman, and any out-of-town guests to gather for an intimate celebration—and a final breather before the wedding.

Customarily, this party is hosted and paid for by the bridegroom's parents. They usually take this time to toast the bride and bridegroom and thank the bride's family (who have traditionally shouldered the rest of the wedding cost).

The rehearsal dinner is a good time to go over any last-minute details or instructions before the wedding and to remind everyone when they should be dressed and in their places for the ceremony. The rehearsal party may be held in a club, restaurant, country inn, or at the home of the bridegroom's parents. If the budget is limited and the list of ushers and attendants long, an informal party, picnic, or simple dessert-and-champagne buffet may be appropriate.

According to traditional etiquette, the bride and bridegroom sit next to each other at the rehearsal dinner—which marks the last time (other than at the wedding) they'll formally do so at a social occasion.

Chapter Six

Dressing the Bride and Attendants

Here comes the bride! All eyes are on you as you glide down the aisle,
so here's when you'll want to look and feel truly radiant.
Choose a dress they won't soon forget.

What does your dream dress look like? Does it have a ball-gown skirt and lacy

bodice? Or is it a sophisticated sheath with uncluttered lines?

Contemporary brides are fortunate, because these days anything goes.

Most brides favor the traditional look of a long white gown, and even women who don't usually gush at beading or frothy lace indulge themselves when it comes to their wedding dress.

But don't feel pressured to dress like a fairy-tale princess if that's not your personal style. There are lots of alternatives: a smart-looking suit, the sophisticated jacket-and-dress ensemble, a snappy miniskirt, or a long white gown with understated details. When I shopped for my own wedding gown, I spent most of the time asking bridal shop owners if they could take the flounces and beads *off* the dress. I wanted a white gown in a luscious fabric with simple lines (no beads, pearls, cabbage roses, or cutouts, thank you). After describing my vision to the umpteenth saleswoman, she smiled and said, "We've got that!" Then she brought out from a storeroom a silk satin gown, and announced that I had actually chosen a debutante's dress. I didn't care what the dress was called—I had finally found IT.

In wedding planning, the gown is the centerpiece choice. Basically, everything is built around it. The gown sets the style and level of formality for the ceremony and reception. That means the bride has to complete her shopping tasks before the rest of the wedding party can begin theirs.

Allow yourself plenty of time for shopping. Most brides shop first for the gown and then choose the coordinating headpiece, accessories, shoes, hose, and jewelry.

THE SEARCH BEGINS

Buying a wedding gown is really a lopsided investment—so much money for a dress worn for so little time. Nationally, the average cost of a wedding gown is around $800–$900, so a wedding gown may be the single most expensive dress purchase a woman ever makes. Designer gowns can run a couple of thousand dollars, and couture gowns (truly one-of-a-kind creations made to fit like a second skin) can cost much, much more. Add the average-priced headpiece (around $150 to $300), shoes (at least $50), and accessories, and the bridal ensemble is a substantial investment.

Most brides-to-be are surprised to learn there is tremendous variation in the quality of wedding-gown fabrics and construction. Spend a thousand dollars on an everyday dress and you're sure to get flawless construction and fabrics to die for. Unfortunately, this isn't necessarily true for wedding wear. Brides are often disappointed at the shoddy construction and downright chintzy fabrics in some gowns. Comparison-shop! Just remember that it is possible to find well-made gowns at every price, so don't settle for something you aren't absolutely in love with.

Since most wedding gowns are custom-fitted, you will need to order the gown at least four to eight months in advance to allow time for the manufacturer to make your dress to the closest size, based on the designer's measurement chart. Fittings and alterations come after delivery to the store, and they usually cost extra. "Keep in mind," says New Jersey bridal consultant Benita Foresta, "that in your gown you'll have to be able to hug, lift and swing your arms, dance, sit, and throw a bouquet!"

Each designer has a different measurement chart, so don't be surprised if you wear a size 10 in one designer's gown and a size 12 in another. Also, many bridal styles are sized smaller than everyday dresses. That means if your regular size is an 8, you may need a 10 for a wedding gown.

Why such a long lead time for ordering?

Once you place an order, the shop sends it to the manufacturer/designer. Many designers wait until they have received a certain number of orders for the same style and size. It's more cost effective for them that way, because they can cut the fabric for multiple dresses at the same time using high-tech pattern-cutting machines. Some designers have speedy turnaround times of several weeks. Others take months. Some manufacturers offer rush service—for a hefty extra charge.

After the gown comes in, allow at least a month for alterations and fittings (which, remember, cost extra). If you plan to wear the gown for a bridal portrait sitting, you'll need it hemmed and in hand at least six weeks before the wedding. (See how far in advance this all takes place?)

A good place to begin shopping is by thumbing through the pages of bridal magazines for pictures of gowns you favor. Note the issue date and dress designer and make a folder of various styles and details. Bring it with you when shopping in order to give the retailer a visual image of what you're looking for. ("I love this illusionary neckline, this kind of pleated hem, and this cap sleeve.")

Most shops require that brides make an appointment for a try-on session. It's helpful to develop a relationship with a knowledgeable retailer who can give you undivided attention and assist you slipping in and out of gowns. (Wedding gowns are often big and unwieldy—you'll need help.) Bring along one friend or relative whose opinion you value, *not* the entire bridal party.

A good way to narrow the search is to try on different silhouettes. The silhouette means the gown's overall shape and line (long and full, short and tapered, and so on). Once you've settled on a flattering dress shape, determine the shade of white you favor. Shades range from ivory, ecru, beige, hospital white, or blush to the palest pink and peach. Next, narrow the choice down to gowns with the details you love (beading, bustle, sweetheart neckline, and so on).

Classic bridal silhouettes abound:

Ball Gown Picture Cinderella: full skirt, off-the-shoulder bodice, and a natural waist.

Sheath A snug, body-hugging look without a waist. The skirt is straight.

A-Line A fitted bodice, gradually flaring wider from the bust down to the hem (just like the shape of the letter A).

Empire Picture those dresses women wore at the time of Napoleon: cropped bodice, very high waist (begins just below the bust), with a slim, slightly flared skirt.

Blouson Loose, drooping draped look from shoulder to waist; gathered at waist.

Princess Slim-fitting bodice that accents the waist, with vertical seams flowing from the shoulders down to the hem of a flared skirt.

Basque Waist Dress waistline begins several inches below the natural waist and snugly forms a curved U-shape or pointed V-shape.

Miniskirt Dress hem falls above the knee.

An experienced retailer will help you find a look that's flattering to your height, weight, and body type. By choosing a gown that accentuates your best features, it will automatically draw attention from less-than-perfect ones. Even supermodels use this fashion trick.

The salesperson should also help you choose the proper undergarments, educate you about the gown's fabric and care requirements, and recommend a flattering headpiece. Be wary of salespeople who gush that every gown "looks perfect" on you; they may be working on commission and too eager to make a sale.

Choose three gowns in a silhouette you love and try on all of them. A wedding dress on a hanger looks completely different than it does on a body.

"Ninety percent of the time, a bride will have an idea of the gown style she wants and sticks with it. When a bride puts on the right one, she smiles automatically. I have seen it time after time. When the mother starts crying and the daughter starts crying, you know she has made the right choice."

—Benita Foresta, New Jersey wedding consultant and
bridal-shop retailer

Flatter Me, Please

The A-line dress flatters most every body type, and the sheath looks wonderful on anyone with a well-proportioned figure. Another flatter-everyone style is the dropped basque waist. "The average woman, whether size 4 or 24, will look dynamite in a dropped basque waist," says consultant Benita Foresta. "It gives a woman a perfect hourglass shape."

Tall and slender brides look good in dresses with flared skirts, wide sashes, raglan sleeves, or low necklines.

Petite? Look for princess shapes and sheaths that lend height. Avoid large ruffles and a bustle. Many designers offer petite lines of gowns featuring properly scaled details: smaller roses and bows, skirts with less volume. The loose, comfortable empire silhouette tends to lengthen the look.

The most slenderizing dress for most body types is the dropped torso with a basque waistline.

Full-figured? An open neckline or lots of embroidery near the neck will draw attention up to the face. Consider a ball-gown skirt, basque waist, long sleeves, and V-neck or boat neckline.

To minimize wide hips, choose a dropped V-waist, flared skirt, or A-line.

To minimize heavy arms, choose leg-of-mutton sleeves that taper toward the elbow. Avoid sleeveless or strapless gowns.

To lengthen a short torso, choose a gown with a wedding-band collar (a stand-up band that circles the neck).

Flat-chested women look wonderful in strapless or sleeveless dresses and dresses with gathers, beading, lacework, or other detailing at the bodice top.

To minimize a large bust, avoid empire styles and clingy fabrics, as well as a heavily decorated bodice. Consider sleeves with a natural shoulder line and a flattering V-neck, or a keyhole yoke neckline that draws attention to the face.

To accentuate curving shoulders and graceful arms, choose a portrait or off-the-shoulder neckline. To highlight a lovely neck, look for a dress with an interesting collar.

WHERE TO SHOP?

Wedding gowns are available in bridal salons, department stores, consignment stores, warehouse outlet stores, and some specialty clothing chains such as Laura Ashley. It's also possible to rent a wedding gown (and bridesmaids' dresses) or to find fabulous new and vintage styles in consignment shops.

Think carefully about how much service you want and expect.

Warehouse and off-price outlets are far cheaper than full-service bridal salons, because the shopper is basically on her own: The gowns are sold off the rack, with no special ordering involved. Once a bride selects her dress, she can take it home with her that day.

Warehouse chains are able to slash prices because they keep lean sales staffs, offer few services, and often buy the gowns in bulk or purchase designer samples or past season styles. Some specialize in "designer look" gowns that mimic the current styles but are constructed in less expensive fabrics and trims. You may be required to pay in full at the time of sale. Be sure to check out the exchange and returns policy and alteration fees. If purchasing a discontinued or sample gown, examine it carefully for signs of damage or stains.

A full-service salon typically offers individualized attention, plus salespeople to help you try on the gowns and coordinate the accessories and headpiece. Many salons now offer the one-stop shopping experience too, where it's possible to buy shoes, hose, jewelry, gown, accessories, makeup, and bridesmaids' attire in one fell swoop without leaving the store. Expect to leave at least a 50 percent deposit at a full-service salon.

Handy Tip:
Think twice about leaving deposits on gowns all over town. Deposits are generally nonrefundable.

Pitfalls to Avoid

❂ Some bridal retailers remove the tags from their gowns so that consumers don't know the name of the manufacturer. This is sometimes a ploy to keep you from comparison shopping and ordering it for less elsewhere. If price is a factor, you might consider taking your business elsewhere.

❀ If the shop has not been in business for a long time, check to see if any complaints have been filed against it with the Better Business Bureau. We've all heard horror stories of brides who plunked down hefty deposits only to find the shop mysteriously closed or the owner gone just days before the wedding.

❀ Pay with a credit card. That way you will have more recourse if there is a problem later. A federal law now protects deposits and payments made with credit cards. If you paid with a credit card and the vendor doesn't provide the goods or services promised, you may be able to withhold full payment until the matter has been settled. (Check with your credit card company, since there are restrictions.)

NECKLINES, SLEEVES, LACES, AND FABRICS

Necklines

Gown details make all the difference. Explaining your vision of the perfect dress is often easier if you know the bridal fashion lingo.

Jewel This neckline circles the base of the neck and is dropped slightly below the throat in front (basically, it falls where a necklace might fall).

Sweetheart Features a front neckline formed like the top half of a heart.

Boat Follows the curving collarbone from shoulder to shoulder in front and back.

Portrait A neckline that stands away from neckbones and shoulder caps. It wraps around the shoulders, gathering at a point just above the bustline in the center front (hence it "frames" the face, like a portrait). If a decorative panel or lace is attached, it forms a Bertha collar. Portrait collars are pretty, but they may inhibit your movements a little.

Fichu Similar to the portrait collar but envelops more of the shoulders with a shawl-like effect. This look was popular on 1950s cocktail dresses.

Square A neckline that dips in front in a half-square shape.

Off-the-Shoulder The dress has sleeves, but the neckline falls below the shoulders and hovers above the bustline.

V-Neck The neckline angled to a point in front.

Keyhole A neckline with an open teardrop shape in front.

Queen Anne Rises high at the back of the neck, then sculpts low in the front in a sweetheart shape or a shape to outline bareness at the upper chest.

Queen Elizabeth Forms a high collar at the back of the neck and comes to a pointed V shape in the front.

Illusionary A neckline that features transparent fabric covering the shoulders in back and the yoke in front.

Sleeve Styles

Balloon Very full, billowy sleeve that ends at the elbow.

Juliet Long sleeve with a poufed top, fitted around the lower arm and wrist.

Gauntlet Detachable lace or fabric sleeve that covers the forearm and wrist.

Cap Short, fitted sleeve that barely covers the top of the arm.

Leg-of-Mutton Awful name for a pretty sleeve featuring a full, rounded look from the shoulder to just above the elbow, then a tapered look from the elbow to the wrist.

Pouf Short, full sleeve gathered at the shoulder. Some pouf sleeves have elastic at the hem and may be worn on or off the shoulder.

Lace

Why are wedding gowns traditionally encrusted with lace? Surprisingly, the answer has to do with medieval commerce and history, notes author and fashion photographer Larry Goldman.

In his book *Dressing the Bride*, Goldman notes that the art of lacemaking began when thrift-conscious medieval women knotted frayed sleeve or hem threads together to prolong the life of an old garment. The practice blossomed from a cottage craft to big-time commerce, and each region (particularly in Brussels, Antwerp, and Venice) became known for its own special designs. Eventually, as lace became regarded as a symbol of affluence and power, it was reserved exclusively for royalty and the clergy.

By the 16th century, "sumptuary" laws were passed restricting when and where people could be seen in public wearing lace! Brides were excluded from this restriction and so took advantage of that one special day to adorn themselves with lacy finery. Wearing lots of lace soon became a bridal tradition.

Today, most laces are made by machine and are categorized by flat or raised designs. Reembroidered lace means a design has been embroidered or embellished on top of the lace for a lush, dimensional look. There are various kinds of laces:

Alençon lace, which originated in France, is one of the most popular bridal laces. This delicate, flat mesh lace features designs on sheer net fabric, outlined with heavy thread or cord.

Chantilly lace which originated in Chantilly, France, features hexagonal mesh and scroll, branch, or floral designs, outlined with scalloped edges. Chantilly lace is very soft and drapes well.

Brussels lace has a cordonnet (heavy thread) edging.

Venise (or Venice) is a heavy raised embroidered lace with a three-dimensional floral or geometric motif. Sections are punched out and then woven with fine threads and thick cording.

Battenberg lace is made from coarse threads and features wide, open loopy designs caught by twisted bars.

Point d'Esprit ("lace of spirit") is characterized by patterns of dots woven into fine net fabric.

Schiffli is man-made lace in which delicate embroidery designs (swags, garlands, or scalloped edging) are worked directly into the fabric.

99

Did You Know . . . ?
Lace motifs or patterns are joined by bars called "brides."

Wedding Gown Fabrics

Stiff, sheer, silky, smooth, or shiny? Take your pick: bridal gown fabrics vary enormously in their drape, texture, and feel.

Taffeta A crisp, shiny cloth with a crosswise rib (often used for bridesmaids' gowns).

Linen A durable, lustrous cloth made from flax.

Moiré A silk taffeta with subtle wavy designs.

Crinoline A stiff fabric used for underskirts.

Shantung An irregularly textured plain-weave silk or man-made fiber.

Faille A heavy, crisp, flat-ribbed fabric of silk or rayon.

Chintz A cotton material with a slightly shiny glazed finish.

Brocade A heavy fabric with interwoven raised designs; includes damask (featuring a reversible figured pattern) and jacquard (a variegated weave with a medallion pattern). Silk brocade is stiff and regal looking.

Sheer fabrics are a world all their own:

Illusion A silk tulle or nylon material popular for veils and necklines.

Chiffon A sheer cotton fabric with a smooth, soft finish.

Organza An almost transparent soft fabric with a stiffer finish than chiffon.

Organdy Sheer and transparent fabric.

Batiste A finely textured sheer cotton or cotton-linen blend.

Voile A very light and soft fabric.

For a smooth, silky look and feel, consider one of the following:

Jersey A soft, fluid fabric that drapes well and is made from wool, rayon, or silk.

Silk A highly prized natural fabric now available in many weights and man-made blends. Look for silk brocade (a full-bodied fabric), silk satin (firm but draping), or silk chiffon (sheer).

Satin Made from silk or synthetic fabric, it has a lustrous, shiny surface. Silk satin is glossy on the front and has a rich, antique-looking sheen. Slipper satin is a lightweight satin made mostly of synthetic material.

Back Interest

Keep in mind that a bride spends much of the ceremony with her back to the guests. Gown back treatments include the bustle and the train. A bustle is a vintage design element dating back to the Middle Ages, when bustles were cages of fabric worn behind the waist to emphasize and extend the woman's figure. This whole cumbersome business was designed to make a woman look more feminine!

Today, many wedding gowns featuring a train—a long swath of material trailing behind the gown—are "bustled" at the waist back for the reception, whereby the train is lifted and tucked or folded into place using a system of drawstrings, hooks, loops, or buttons.

Trains may hang from the shoulders (a watteau train), drape from the waist, or be a continuation of the back hem (a sweeping train). The longer the train, the more formal the look. Among the most popular train lengths:

Cathedral train (from the waist, about three yards long)

Chapel train (about 1⅓ yards long)

Brush train (trails behind the dress, barely touching the floor)

Remember to choose the appropriate train length for your height and weight.

The Crowning Glory

Will you wear a headpiece or veil? Obviously, whatever you choose should coordinate with the gown's silhouette, neckline, fabric, detailing and color. But more important, the headpiece should proportion and frame your face, as well as balance the entire wedding ensemble.

Nowadays, a veil is an elegant accessory, and wearing one is a matter of personal choice. But centuries ago the veil was considered an absolute necessity to protect the bride from evil spirits. In some cultures the bride wore a veil to symbolize purity—or even covered her face during the entire courtship.

When shopping, wear your hair in the style you plan for the wedding day. Experiment with headpieces of different sizes and shapes. Some brides bring along a Polaroid camera for instant snapshots. If you intend to wear contact lenses on the wedding day, wear them while trying on gowns. Obviously, the headpiece's color should match the same white shade as the gown.

Consider which is the most flattering look for you: a headpiece that rests at the back of the head, goes from ear to ear (like a wreath or headband), sits right on top (pillbox or crown), or crosses the forehead.

Brides with less than perfect features should avoid the band across the forehead, as this severe look slices the face in two and exaggerates facial flaws. Headpiece styles have a wide range:

Pillbox Small, flat hat designed to sit either high on the head or slanted to one side.

Wreath Circle of flowers, beading, or crystal sprays that rests on top of the head or across the middle of the forehead.

Headband Puffed or flat strip of fabric that rests in a band across the top of the head.

Juliet Cap A delicate bridal cap that hugs the crown.

Backpiece Bow, barrette, or hair ornament worn at the back of the head (or high up on the head) from which a veil is often attached.

Tiara Princess-style crown made from real or faux stones.

Picture Hat Large, with a wide, glamorous brim.

Garden Hat Crownless hat that is often trimmed with flowers.

Mantilla Lace or netting that is attached to a raised comb framing the face with lovely folds.

Profile—A headpiece spray of flowers, pearls, or other decoration usually worn on an angle, on one side of the head.

The most common veil lengths:

Fingertip Comes down to the tips of the fingers.

Blusher Worn over the face and falls to the collarbone (or as low as the waist).

Ballet or Waltz Length Falls to slightly below the knee.

Sweep veil Barely skims the ground.

Chapel Extends beyond the gown up to two feet.

Royal An ultraformal length that spills two yards along the ground.

Some brides prefer to remove the traditional veil and headpiece at the reception and replace it with a smaller wreath (or shorter veil) that is easier to wear while dancing.

"If budget is something you are concerned with, I would recommend consignment shops that deal in formal wear. I am probably saving at least $700 by going this route. You can find modern styles as well as antique vintage clothing, and sometimes the shop will scout out gowns for you. In a consignment shop, I found a 1940s Victorian-style silk dress that has aged to a beautiful ivory color. It's gorgeous!"

—Elizabeth Mushinksy, Connecticut September bride

Jewelry and Accessories

Bridal jewelry should complement rather than compete with the wedding gown or ensemble.

Understated jewelry styles have traditionally been the bridal standard, because brides tend to choose fewer but more heirloom-quality pieces for wedding wear. As a result, bridal jewelry tends to be more formal than funky. If your family has a real tiara, heirloom cameo, or antique broach, this may be the time to display it. (You'll be satisfying the "something old" custom at the same time.)

When choosing jewelry, keep in mind the general tone and style of the wedding, as well as the gown neckline, silhouette, and fabric.

Pearls are always the perfect complement to a wedding gown and also symbolize happiness. Pearls come in shades of white, ecru, and blush pink and can be chosen to flatter every complexion color.

A simple rule of thumb: The more ornate the gown, the simpler the jewelry should be.

Jewelry for a daytime wedding should be less dramatic or opulent (simple studs or a delicate necklace) than for an ultraformal evening wedding (tiaras and dripping diamonds).

For an informal or country wedding, a gold or silver locket may be appropriate.

For a high-necked gown or one with lots of beading or lace just below the face, a fussy necklace will overdo the look. Instead, make a statement with simple stud earrings or clustered earrings with pearls or crystals chosen to match or mirror the beadwork in the gown.

Some brides choose to move their engagement ring to the right hand until after the ceremony (to make slipping on the wedding ring easier). It's also wise to avoid wearing any ring on the right hand during the receiving line, when it's necessary to shake hands for a long time.

A bride should never feel pressured to wear a piece of heirloom jewelry on her wedding day just because her mother-in-law or another loved one wants her to for sentimental reasons.

Gloves Look for decorative wrist ornaments and beading, lacy fabrics and styles with the fingertips snipped off. Long gloves are an elegant complement to a gown with little or no sleeve. With a short sleeve, choose a short glove. A sleeveless gown or gown with elbow-length sleeves looks lovely with elbow-length gloves.

Handbag Choose a small bag for necessities only. Look for decorative fabrics or beading to complement the gown. Ask your maid or matron of honor to hold onto it for you at the reception.

Makeup

The wedding day is not the time to experiment with makeup. Just ask New York wedding photographer Wendy Stewart, who recalls a bride who used a new brand of makeup on her wedding day and broke out in an awful splotchy rash. The makeup artist promptly removed it, but it took several hours for the bride's face to "calm down," and it delayed the wedding ceremony and portrait taking.

Makeup consultant Laura Torres Hodgins suggests brides seek a consultation with a professional makeup artist before the wedding. A professional makeup application ($20–$50) can make a significant difference in the way the bride looks and how the wedding photographs turn out.

"Don't deviate much from what you wear on a day-to-day basis," counsels Hodgins. "Someone who doesn't wear makeup ever will want something to enhance her appearance, while someone who wears a lot should realize makeup must never be overpowering. You don't want people to say, 'Did you see her makeup?' when you walk down the aisle."

When applying makeup, be sure your gown is covered with a smock or cloth. To avoid stains, apply makeup first, cover the face with a cloth or pillowcase, and then slip the gown over your head.

Hodgins suggests the following tips for wedding makeup:

- Tell the makeup artist the time and location of the wedding and how it's going to be recorded (with photographer or videographer).

❀ Make sure the eye colors are matte (not shiny or reflective), because a camera flash will bounce off the iridescent pigment.

❀ The face should be well powdered.

❀ To ensure lipstick lasts throughout talking and toasting, use a lip liner to outline the lips and again to fill in the lips with color. Then apply lipstick on top of the liner. (Lip liner is less waxy than lipstick.) Blot, reapply the lipstick, and blot again.

❀ Lips and eyes should be well defined. Eyeliner will give nice definition to the eyes.

❀ Avoid too much blush.

107

DRESSING THE BRIDESMAIDS

Bridesmaids' dresses get a bad rap.

No wonder. Bridal attendants often grouse that once the wedding's over, they will never wear their dresses again. Where else but a wedding could you show up in a taffeta Cinderella skirt and pouf sleeves, wearing shoes dyed the color of an Easter egg? It's not surprising so many bridesmaid dresses end up on garage-sale racks or used as Halloween costumes.

The good news: Fashion designers have finally responded to the collective groans and are creating dresses that can double as cocktail or special-occasion attire.

At long last you can select from sophisticated sheaths, handsome lacy suits, and glamorous gowns that are anything but frumpy or matronly. Many of the newest looks feature tasteful bareness and body-hugging styles that reflect the trend toward fitness and toned bodies.

The bride will want to shop with her attendants and suggest her preferences, but the final decision still rests with her. Since the bridesmaids pay for their own dresses, a thoughtful bride will be considerate of their tastes and choices. When shopping for dresses, it's important that everyone in the wedding party visit the same shop or salon. To ensure the same dye lots and details, place one order for the entire group at the same time.

Don't feel restricted to bridal-shop offerings. If the bridesmaids live all over the country, consider shopping by mail-order catalogue, in department stores, or in specialty chains like Laura Ashley with branches nationwide.

The only rule of thumb is that while bridesmaid dresses may be shorter than the bride's, they are never longer. The dresses need not be identical, but for a harmonious look walking down the aisle, choose dresses in a similar style and color.

The challenge of choosing a flattering bridesmaid style is that wedding parties come in different shapes and sizes. The problem can be sidestepped by selecting a two-piece ensemble so that you can more easily adjust the top and bottom to the different measurements.

Color is another important factor. Ever wonder why so many bridesmaids wear pink or peach? It's because those two colors flatter just about anybody.

Sophisticated colors like black, white, or navy can easily be worn again.

(Yes, Virginia, it's now okay for bridesmaids to wear white, just like the bride, or to wear black, which was once considered bad luck.)

For even more fashion mileage, choose a cocktail dress with a detachable sheer overskirt. Another smart choice is a floor-length two-piece suit (dress or skirt with jacket) that can later be trimmed to knee length for evening wear. The simpler and less decorated a floor-length dress is, the more opportunities there will be for multiple uses. A classic ankle-length sheath in brocade or a fabric spun with gold or silk thread looks smashing when cut down.

Choosing flattering styles for a pregnant attendant is no longer a problem. Many dress manufacturers now carry maternity lines for bridesmaids that use the same fabrics and colors used for special occasion dresses. You may wish to order extra fabric for alterations. It's often difficult to determine a pregnant woman's final size several months hence. If need be, the dress can be enlarged with special seams and gussets.

109

THE MOTHERS

Think total look. The mothers of the bride and groom will be wise to choose outfits that complement the look of the bridesmaids. (Again, think how everyone will look standing next to each other in photographs.)

Generally, the mother of the bride chooses her outfit first, and then the bridegroom's mother selects something in a complementary style and color. If one mom insists on a short dress and another wants to wear long, remind them how lopsided it will look in the wedding album.

Unless the entire wedding party will be wearing black, or the wedding style is particularly sophisticated, talk your mother out of choosing an all-black outfit. Until recently, black was taboo for weddings. Even today, in some cultures the bride's mother wearing black means she is a recent widow or doesn't approve of the marriage. On the other hand, the right black dress can be chic and elegant for an evening wedding.

CHILD ATTENDANTS

Choose styles in keeping with the child's age. That means saying no to peek-a-boo backs for junior bridesmaids and yes to ankle-length skirts for little flower-girls who might trip on floor-sweeping hems.

The child attendants need not be dressed identically to the older attendants (or they'll look like they are playing dress-up), but choose fabrics and colors that are complementary. Often the flower girl's dress echoes the bride's and incorporates the same lace, neckline, or poufy sleeves.

For children, comfort is key. If you want them to look presentable and precious, pick outfits they won't want to tear off at the first chance. That means no scratchy underskirts or headpieces that pinch; that means comfortable shoes. When your flower girl tries on a dress, ask if it feels heavy. Sound silly? Many styles with crinolines and yards of fabric are too downright heavy for a small child to wear all day. Remember to dress her at the very *last* minute, and ask the child's mother to bring along an extra pair of tights or pantyhose and spare hair bow. It's a fact: Kids will run and play even in wedding clothes. (See also "Children at the Wedding," chapter 11.)

WHAT WILL THE MEN WEAR?

Clothes for the men in the wedding party (including the bridegroom and his father) are traditionally governed by time of day of the wedding.

All the men wear the same attire, except for the accessories. The bridegroom and best man can jazz up their outfits with matching ties and, if tuxedos are worn, cummerbunds. The bride and bridegroom sometimes coordinate their accessories too! The bridegroom may wear a tartan cummerbund or tie to match the bride's tartan waistband or the colored ribbons in her bouquet.

Any bridegroom who needs to wear a tuxedo two or three times a year is wise to buy, rather than rent, a wedding tuxedo. The average tuxedo rental package includes the tux, shirt, cummerbund, bow tie, and shoes.

Save yourself a lot of aggravation by reminding all the men to check the pieces in their rental package before taking it out of the shop. Horror stories abound of ushers who walk down the aisle in borrowed tennis shoes because they never opened the rental-wear box until arriving at the ceremony venue.

According to the International Formalwear Association based in Chicago, the name *tuxedo* actually comes from Tuxedo Park, New York, a hunting resort built in 1886 for the wealthy. The story goes that when a Tuxedo Park socialite couple named Potter visited England on holiday, they attended a royal court ball where they were introduced to the Prince of Wales (who later became King Edward VII). The prince was captivated by Mrs. Potter's beauty and invited them both for a weekend at his country house. When her husband confided to the future king that he didn't know what proper English gentlemen wore on such occasions, the prince admitted that he had recently begun wearing a short black jacket, instead of the customary formal coat with long tails in the back. Mr. Potter had a short jacket made on the spot. When he returned to Tuxedo Park and began wearing it to society functions, the short jacket resembling today's blazer became the rage, and men began referring to it as the "tuxedo" jacket.

Formal-wear customs vary widely across the country. For advice on choosing attire, consult your local formal-wear store or wedding consultant. The International Formalwear Association also offers a free pamphlet, *Your Formalwear Guide*, containing advice on contemporary and traditional fashions and current standards of etiquette. (To receive a copy, send a stamped, self-addressed business-size envelope to the International Formalwear Association, 401 N. Michigan Ave., Chicago, IL 60611.) Excerpts from the pamphlet are reprinted below, with IFA permission.

Groom's Contemporary Attire

Very Formal Evening Wedding

Requires black full dress (tailcoat); white or other color is acceptable. The shirt coordinates with the tailcoat; the tie and vest should match the tailcoat in color, except if wearing black full dress, when it should be a white wing-collar piqué shirt with white piqué vest and bow. Shoes are patent leather.

Very Formal Daytime Wedding

Updated cutaway (usually gray), with striped or matching trousers, white shirt, striped tie or ascot; or tuxedo in conservative colors.

Formal Daytime Wedding

Tuxedo or tailcoat in range of colors (dark for winter, pastels for spring and summer or tropical climate). Updated stroller coat, with striped trousers.

Groom's Traditional Attire

Very Formal Evening Wedding

The groom wears black full dress (tailcoat) with formal white piqué wing-collar shirt, white piqué vest, and bow tie. (A wing collar has little downward points.) Shoes are patent leather.

Very Formal Daytime Wedding

Cutaway coat, gray striped trousers, gray vest, ascot or striped four-in-hand tie (knotted tie that hangs vertically). Optional top hat, spats, gray gloves. Shoes are patent leather.

Semiformal Daytime Wedding

Gray stroller, with striped trousers, pearl gray vest, four-in-hand tie, white pleated formal shirt. Optional: homburg, gloves.

Ushers

Generally, the ushers wear attire similar or identical to the groom's, but with different boutonniere or tie. However, for a contemporary semiformal evening wedding, if the groom chooses a tailcoat, the users can wear similar-color tuxedos. At a very formal evening wedding, the groom and ushers wear identical black full dress (tailcoat) suits.

What do all these formal-wear terms mean?

Tails (or Tailcoat) Refers to a formal coat that is short in front and extends to two long tails in back.

Stroller Coat A semiformal suit jacket cut like a tuxedo and worn during the day.

Cutaway Coat Also called a morning coat; tapers from the waistline button to one wide tail in the back, with a vent.

Tuxedo A short jacket cut almost like a business suit jacket or blazer. It is worn after 6 P.M. to any formal event where the women are in formal clothes. A tuxedo may be single- or double-breasted. If the invitation indicates black tie, this means the tuxedo and trousers should be black, and the accessories, shirt, and vest white.

GOWN PRESERVATION AND CLEANING

Wedding memories may fade over time, but with a little care your wedding gown can remain a prized possession for years to come.

Time isn't the only enemy of a gown. Heat, light, dampness, stains, poor storage conditions, and a plastic environment can also turn a once gorgeous gown into a yellowed, brittle, or faded mess of fibers. Yet these detrimental effects can be curbed with professional care of the gown by a dry cleaner.

Most gowns will turn a pale shade of gold or yellow over time due to the chemical process of oxidation. If you've ever cut an apple in half and left it on a counter, you may have seen it turn brown. That's because oxygen adds to the already present tannin in the apple, causing a chemical change. Over time, fabric reacts in a similar way.

Make arrangements for the cleaning and preservation of the gown long before you leave for the honeymoon. You'll want to wrap the gown in a clean, undyed, unsized, unbleached cotton sheet right after taking it off. So before the wedding, purchase a white cotton sheet with as little synthetic fiber content as possible and wash it in hot water (with no detergent) to remove any dirt and sizing.

Never store the gown in a plastic bag after wearing it, because plastics decompose, giving off fumes that cause rapid oxidation of the textile and deposit acidic residues on the fabric, explains Christine Morrissey, president of National Gown Cleaners, a gown-cleaning and preservation company based in San Jose, California. Morrissey suggests the bride assign a loved one to wrap the gown and take it to a cleaner within the first thirty days after wearing; the sooner the better. The longer stains sit, the less chance there is of removing them, creating a risk to the fabric.

Place the gown on top of a cotton sheet and then roll it loosely or wrap it, keeping it as flat as possible, away from sunlight and areas that are moist or damp, until a decision is made where to take it.

Choose a dry cleaner carefully. Morrissey suggests asking the following questions:

1. How many gowns do you handle on the average per year?

2. Do you have a dry cleaner formally trained in the business of stain removal?

3. How long have you been in business?

4. Do you have letters of referral?

Be sure to tell the dry cleaner exactly where the stains are and what caused them. ("There is a perspiration stain under the arm, and we spilled salad dressing near the hem.") Be sure you know the fiber content of the gown and the types of beading used. Beads should be secured and sewn on before cleaning.

There are several routes to preservation. Some brides prefer vacuum-sealed box storage, which involves cleaning the gown (either by dry cleaning, water cleaning, or a combination of both) and then storing in a sturdy box from which the air has been removed, leaving a virtual vacuum. Before the gown is boxed, it is wrapped in acid-free tissue paper (because acid accelerates the deterioration process).

An alternative to the sealed preservation box is to have the gown professionally cleaned and then stored in an unbleached cotton sheet. Before hanging, the gown bodice is stuffed with acid-free tissue paper to prevent wrinkles (which will set over time and damage the fibers).

Critics of the sealed vacuum box and hanging methods insist the gown should be stored in only archival-quality tissue paper, in an archival-quality box, and refolded occasionally over the years. (They argue that vacuum-sealed storage traps in moisture, which can lead to mildew, and that most boxes used for this type of storage have plastic windows. They note, moreover, that hanging a garment places irreversible strain and damage on the fabric over time.

Morrissey suggests storing the gown in an acid-free, lignin-free box that meets specifications for archival preservation—that is, it meets the high standards for materials used by museums and textile conservationists. These materials are available from some dry cleaners. Acid-free unbuffered or buffered tissue should be used in between the folds of the gown to prevent permanent breaks or wrinkles. (For a synthetic gown, use buffered archival paper; for a natural fiber gown, unbuffered paper.) Remove fabric-covered metal buttons, pins, and sponge padding, and store them separately. Metal trims could oxidize and stain the fabric; some padding materials can yellow with age. Store the gown in a dry place, away from heat and moisture (not the attic or the basement).

Take the gown out of the box and refold and inspect it every five to seven years. Wear white gloves to prevent oily fingers from damaging the fabric. Air should circulate around the box and provide a consistent, stable environment in which the gown ages.

Brides with an eye to preserving their gown for future generations are wise to select a wedding gown in an all-natural fabric such as cotton or silk. If stored with care, a gown with no trace of synthetic fibers will last longer than will one with man-made fibers. When my grandmother celebrated her sixtieth wedding anniversary, she took her 1920s silk sheath dress out of a box where it had been lovingly stored in special archival paper, and then slipped it on. It still fit. Grandma had kept her slim figure over the years, and the dress had retained its beauty, mellowing from a bright white to a candlelight ivory. The dress was sixty. She was eighty. They both looked lovely.

Chapter Seven

The Wedding Cake

Think delicious! Think dramatic! Take a bite of the sweetest wedding tradition of all. It's hard to imagine a wedding celebration without the three main ingredients: a bride, a groom, and a wedding cake.

The wedding cake is a showpiece dessert and the dramatic conclusion to a celebration feast. But this vision in buttercream is more than just a tribute to the baker's architectural prowess. The cake holds a place of honor at the reception, since the cake-cutting ceremony is a highlight of any wedding celebration. The wedding cake is also a symbol of happiness, good fortune, and a sweet life together.

Legend has it that wedding cakes are traditionally tiered because guests once brought sweet buns as gifts to the couple. As guests arrived, these little breads or cakes would be heaped into a large stack, shaped like a tower.

The art of the wedding cake reached its heyday in the stylized Victorian era, notes artist and master baker Collette Peters in *Collette's Wedding Cakes*. Peters says today's classic wedding-cake look (tiers festooned with decoration) evolved from the Victorians' sentimental view of love and their love of ornament.

Three-tiered cakes remain the traditional standard, and many brides choose a butter or sponge cake with creamy white filling and white or ivory buttercream frosting piped into lacy swirls and rosettes.

The tiers can be stacked one on top of another or separated by sturdy columns and discs designed to keep the cake balanced and stable. How does it all keep from toppling? To ensure the bottom layers support the weight of the tiers, wooden dowels are often inserted into each tier to distribute the weight.

But say good-bye to the image of dry white cake with bland, tasteless frosting. These days, couples want cakes that both make a fabulous impression and taste wonderful. Which means they often choose their favorite—be it chocolate mousse, cheesecake, or carrot cake.

Just about any cake can be made into a wedding cake—sponge cake, butter cake, chocolate cake, cheesecake, pound cake, fruitcake, genoise, meringue layers, or even cream puffs. A recent winter bride astonished her guests with a croquembouche wedding cake formed from a tower of piled profiteroles (cream puffs) and wrapped in a glistening sheath of caramelized spun sugar.

Decorations are limited only by the bride's imagination and the baker's artistic skill. Flourishes can include anything from icing flowers dipped in gold or multicolored powders to roses handcrafted from real gold leaf, not to mention basketweave frosting designs, lacy dotted-swiss effects, chocolate ruffles, and fabric ribbons or gold cording pressed into the side of the cake.

Real flowers or cascading green ivy add a burst of color to traditional white or pastel cakes, and some cakes even include gauzy fabric sprays or ribbons (to match the bride's gown) tucked in between the layers.

And the shape is no longer limited to the imposing tiered tower. Master bakers are making wedding cakes shaped like top hats, convertibles, four-poster beds, cloisonné bells, Fabergé eggs—or whatever else the couple fancies.

Bakers can make remarkable floral decorations that are stunningly realistic —and edible, too! Using gum paste, royal icing, or sugar molds, they can fashion flowers so delicate and lifelike they seem fresh plucked from nature. Susan Morgan, owner of Elegant Cheesecakes in Half Moon Bay, California specializes in designs made of imported chocolate. She has created amazingly lifelike tiger lily blossoms, roses, and orchids from chocolate rolled paper thin, fashioned into individual petals, tinted with edible food coloring, and assembled into blooms.

Today, cakes are often decorated to reflect the bride's gown, the wedding colors, or even the season of the celebration. Morgan often makes flower-pot-shaped cakes that double as edible centerpieces. Wrapped in terra-cotta-colored chocolate, they look just like plants!

In addition to the tiered look, popular wedding-cake shapes include the sheet cake, single-layer round cake, heart-shaped cake, or sculpted look created by displaying the layers on different-height pedestals on the table. "We did one where the cake was designed as a stack of gift boxes," says Rich Ringelstein of

Colonial Caterers in Napierville, Illinois. "Each box had a different frosting, so it looked like a different gift."

Can't decide on a favorite flavor? Give guests a choice. Ask the baker to prepare different cakes for each layer, perhaps one tier of chocolate, one of carrot, and another of white butter cake. It satisfies everybody, and the three-cakes-in-one confection is visually striking when cut.

WHERE TO BEGIN?

Cake costs are usually calculated by the serving. Expect to spend between $1 and $10 per slice, although designer cakes requiring time-consuming hand decoration and special ingredients can run thousands of dollars. Most of the expense for a wedding cake is *labor-related*. Many couples are surprised to learn that special frills like spun-sugar flowers or chocolate roses are billed by the individual decoration, so a cake with a "bouquet" of handpainted details will cost precipitously more than one with a few blooms here and there.

Order a cake at least six months in advance and arrange for a taste test. Most bakers will offer a taste test, although you may have to schedule it for a day when they are already baking for another special event.

DELICIOUS DETAILS:
QUESTIONS TO ASK THE BAKER

Be sure to ask whether the cake will be fresh or previously frozen, how it will be transported (some bakers insist the client picks up the cake at the shop), and whether it will be assembled at the reception site. Ask if the baker uses only fresh ingredients or whether prepared industrial cake mixes or dyes are employed. Also, if you want a truly white cake, find out what kind of butter is used. Butters range from sunny yellow to pale ivory, and a buttercream frosting made with bright yellow butter may not produce the true white shade you'd hoped for.

Many tiered cakes, unless simply stacked, should be transported in layers and assembled and decorated on site to prevent disasters. Ask the baker if there are extra charges for assembly, delivery, cake plates, columns, and separators. If the cake is delivered to the reception, make sure someone you trust is there to receive and inspect it ("No, we didn't order a pink cake with a Minnie Mouse cake topper!"), and later baby-sit it so it doesn't get knocked over or bumped. Also, ask if they charge an extra cake-cutting fee (for the labor involved in slicing and serving the cake).

When choosing a design, it's helpful to bring along a swatch from the gown and inform the baker about the wedding colors, theme, number of guests, and location. Believe it or not, the size of the reception site is important to the size of the cake. Consider, for instance, ordering a taller cake (four or even five tiers) for a large ballroom with high ceilings.

The average wedding cake consists of three tiers—twelve, nine, and six inches high—and serves about 125–150 people.

Wedding cake portions are traditionally small because the cake is usually served following a large meal that may include other desserts as well. The serving size is generally a two-inch square or an angled slice two inches wide and three inches high. Be sure to tell the baker whether the cake will be the only dessert served. Keep in mind that in warmer parts of the country, whipped cream, meringue, and ice cream cakes can prove disastrous in the peak summer months, so much so that some bakers will ask you to sign a disclaimer if you insist on these risky ingredients.

Some cakes are more easily sliced than others. This is an important time consideration when serving cake to several hundred people. The problem is easily sidestepped by asking the baker to make a small version for presentation at the reception and several large sheet cakes for slicing behind the scenes.

Some bakers will also prepare a "dummy cake," a styrofoam-based fake cake decorated to look like the real thing. The top tier is often real cake, and the remaining tiers are a kind of specially formulated plastic foam that doesn't splinter or absorb frosting. In certain "wedding palace" hotels in Japan where enormous weddings are staged, dummy cakes are routinely used, and couples can choose from hundreds of models from an elaborate display.

Bakers will sometimes make an extra top layer for the couple to freeze and enjoy on their first anniversary. Since year-old frozen cake can taste mighty nasty, even if carefully wrapped, you might consider asking the baker to prepare a fresh layer for the anniversary. Sometimes the cost of the wedding cake includes a free anniversary layer one year later.

Some couples also choose to serve a groom's cake alongside the wedding cake (often a dense fruity rum cake topped with marzipan or rolled fondant). This tradition dates back to the pioneer days when cakes were baked by the groom's parents for guests to enjoy on their long trip home. It was believed that single guests who slept with a wrapped slice of groom's cake under their pillow would dream about a future spouse. Today the groom's cake is served at the reception or packed into tiny boxes for guests to take home as favors.

Another dessert alternative at weddings is the sweets table (sometimes called a Viennese table). This sumptuous buffet of cakes, candies, and pastries is served at the reception as the grand finale to the event, often alongside a cappuccino bar or assortment of liqueurs.

Did You Know . . . ?

❀ Cutting the wedding cake at the reception represents the couple's shared life together. For the cake-cutting ceremony, the bridegroom traditionally puts his right hand on the bride's, and they cut the first slice together.

❀ While couples once relied on porcelain figurines of the bride and groom for cake toppers, the trend is to use flowers, ribbons, or the topper your parents used on their cake.

POPULAR WEDDING CAKE AND FILLING COMBINATIONS

- Fresh carrot cake with cream-cheese frosting.

- Vanilla cake filled with chocolate mousse, or chocolate cake filled with white chocolate mousse. When sliced, these cakes boast a powerful contrasting look. Alternate the layers for even more drama.

- Rum cake with vanilla mousse filling and rum glaze.

- Yellow cake with cheesecake and caramel nut filling.

- Chocolate cake with fresh fruit filling.

- Lemon pound cake with buttercream, raspberry, or lemon mousse filling.

- Cheesecake with apricot or lemon filling.

- Chocolate cake with raspberry filling and mocha ganache.

- Rum-soaked fruitcake with rolled fondant icing.

- Strawberry shortcake with whipped cream.

- Chocolate cake with chocolate mousse filling, wrapped in white chocolate.

- White chocolate cake with lemon mousse and white-chocolate ganache.

Glazes and Frostings:

Traditional Buttercream Can refer to a frosting made from confectioner's sugar and butter or shortening, or a frosting made from egg yolks (or whites), butter, and a boiled sugar syrup. Both pipe easily into designs and swirls.

Flavors include chocolate, mocha, caramel crunch, apricot, chestnut, raspberry, lemon, orange, white chocolate cream cheese, pineapple, and more.

Rolled Fondant Sweet icing (made from corn syrup, confectioner's sugar, and other ingredients) that is rolled out with a rolling pin and literally draped over the cake. Fondant gives cakes a smooth, alabasterlike finish and provides a perfect backdrop for decorations. For a quilted effect, ask your baker to gently roll the tines of a tracing wheel over the fondant. Fondant originated in England and is especially popular in Australia, where dense wedding fruitcakes are the standard.

Ganache A luxurious glaze made from melted chocolate and cream.

Ask Your Baker about These Decorations

- Satin ribbons and French-wired ribbons (these bend into shapes)
- Dragees (silver or gold candy balls)
- Gold and silver leaf (edible real gold or silver available in paper-thin strips)
- Piping gel for stained-glass effects
- Royal icing (a stiff icing used for flowers, fruits, and designs)
- Chocolate curls, ruffles, ribbons, "cigarette" sticks, or leaves
- Meringue mushrooms and swans
- Chocolate gift boxes or place cards
- Molded sugar decorations (basket, cottage, vase)
- Flowers: fresh, silk, or made from royal icing, gum paste, or buttercream

Be sure the fresh flowers you use are of the edible varieties! Edible flowers include lilacs, pansies, petunias, nasturtiums, roses, violets, and apple blossoms. Double-check with the florist before choosing flowers for the cake, or be sure that any nonedible flowers are removed before serving!

Gum Paste Decorations Gum paste is an edible material used by bakers to create unbelievably realistic decorations including shells, fruits, flowers, and branches. Gum paste may be easily formed into loops or bows or rolled out cookie-dough style and cut into shapes with gum paste cutters.

Modeling Chocolate Imagine a cross between Tootsie Rolls and modeling clay. Modeling chocolate is a mixture of chocolate and corn syrup that has a firm, pliable texture. It can be run through a pasta maker to create ruffles and ribbons, or shaped into flowers and leaves.

Marzipan A smooth mixture of almond paste, corn syrup, and sugar, which can be tinted and rolled into sheets or shaped into animals, fruits, or flowers.

Spun Sugar ("Angel's Hair") A web of fine, long crystallized sugar strands. Made by heating sugar and corn syrup to a high temperature (around 360°F.) and then waving fork tines or a balloon whisk (cut at the round end to expose tines) to make the cooling sugar form long amber strands.

Handy Tip:

If cost is a consideration, order an undecorated tiered cake with plain white or pastel frosting. Then arrange for the wedding consultant or someone you trust to bring a few fresh flowers or beautiful ribbons to the reception and press them gently into the sides (you may need to anchor the decoration with toothpicks). Voilà! An inexpensive and gorgeous look—instantly.

Decorative Piping Styles

- dots
- snail trail
- shells
- rope border
- reverse shells
- rosebuds and half rose
- zigzags
- ruffle
- lily of the valley
- fleur-de-lis
- basketweave

Approximate Serving Yields from Standard Pan Sizes

Round Pan

6" serves 10
8" serves 20
10" serves 35
12" serves 50

Square Pan

6" serves 12–15
8" serves 28–30
10" serves 45–50
12" serves 65–70

Sweet Ideas

- Custom-made chocolate place cards featuring the guest's name piped onto a chocolate rectangle or the center of a chocolate blossom. Baker Susan Morgan often coordinates the color of the trim with the entrée the guest has chosen for dinner. (That way the servers know that everyone with, say, a pink-trimmed flower gets salmon; yellow trim means beef.)
- Individual desserts, such as chocolate truffles filled with cream, or meringues and berry sauce.

- Chocolate-dipped strawberries, orange sections, kiwi slices, or other fruits.
- Madeleine sponge cakes dusted with confectioner's sugar.
- Cakes that double as centerpieces.

"My wedding was simple, elegant, and affordable. It was last minute but well organized, and we took only a week or two to plan. We had two wedding cakes, a German cake and a French cake, because we are of French descent. The German cake was a gift from my husband's aunt, who is of German descent. The French-style cake, which had two layers, was a gift from my daughter's godmother. The guests said how beautiful the two cakes were."

—Martine Sixto Wirtemburg, Connecticut March bride

Chapter Eight

Flowers

Flowers are the crowning glory of any wedding.
They lend fragrance and color and define the wedding's unique
personality, be it traditional, romantic, country, or formal.

It's difficult to imagine a bride without a bouquet of lovely flowers. Flowers throughout the ages have been an enduring symbol of love, fertility, and romance and were also believed to ward off evil spirits with their pungent fragrances. (Imagine carrying a bouquet trimmed with garlic, as brides did long ago!)

Flowers can represent a significant slice of a couple's wedding budget—10 to 20 percent—and like the gown, they make a striking visual statement.

While many couples find it hard to rationalize spending large sums on such a pretty but perishable item, consider that flowers breathe life and joy into any celebration and also provide splashes of color and a stunning natural backdrop for the wedding photographs.

WHERE TO BEGIN?

Put yourself in the hands of a talented florist. Like photographers, some florists are more artistic and creative than others. Call ahead and make an appointment to discuss your floral budget and what you have in mind. A good florist will work within any budget or floral scheme. High-priced floral designers who do celebrity parties and charity balls have often told me they will slash their rates for brides who honestly admire their work; or they will work within a tight wedding budget.

Chicago floral designer Virginia Wolff advises choosing a florist who has extensive experience with weddings. "Some florists are geared up to do weddings, while others aren't used to dealing with all the details, the timing, and the delivery of a big party."

How do you find one? Call the catering managers at the three best hotels and three best country clubs in town. Ask for three recommendations from each. One or two names will be on top of *everyone's* list, Wolff says. As you interview florists, you'll get a feel for who tends toward standard "cookbook" designs and who is comfortable working with exotic blooms and loose, unstructured shapes.

Some florists prefer to call themselves floral designers because they work with a larger vocabulary of flowers than others and are experienced with custom designs to transform any space into a floral wonderland. They often carry unusual flowers, special vases, and greenery and will tailor arrangements to the gown or wedding theme. Many floral designers also provide special lighting services, table settings, and themed props, and will create floral or fabric decorations for an arbor, mantel, chuppah, pews, tent, or even the backs of chairs. Wolff often festoons the bride and groom's chairs with lavish bunches of fresh flowers and bows.

Lighting lends special drama and elegance to wedding decorations and flowers. Pinspot lighting involves showcasing just the centerpiece flowers with strategically placed lights. Twinkling lights can be woven among tree branches or draped with tulle fabric along pews. A talented floral designer can often "wrap" unsightly poles or exposed pipes with swaths of romantic tulle or pretty greenery. These easy-to-do touches provide instant magic!

Ask to see a portfolio of the florist's work. Must you choose from standard arrangements in an FTD book, or can you experiment with different stems for a special look? Ask if you can come early to another wedding and take a sneak peak while the florist is setting up.

Be sure to inspect the flowers going out the door. Are they at the peak of freshness, or slightly wilted and discolored? Ask how far ahead of time the arrangements will be assembled and where they'll be stored. Also, ask if the florist will be working on any other weddings that same day.

133

It's also important to stipulate where the flowers will be delivered and when. Some brides prefer the flowers to arrive at home to literally have them in hand before leaving for the ceremony. If the flowers are to be delivered to the ceremony venue, arrange for someone to be there and accept them. And call ahead to ensure the florist has the full address! More than one couple has had the misfortune of learning their flowers were sent to the wrong place.

ROSES OR RANUNCULUSES?

Obviously, the cost of wedding flowers varies dramatically with the blossoms you choose. In-season and locally grown flowers naturally cost less than out-of-season or exotic ones. But these days the flower market is a global one, and most florists have access to fresh-picked flowers from all over the world. The tulips on your table today may be have been plucked from Dutch soil only yesterday.

Order wedding flowers as early as possible—preferably six months to a year before the event. The florist will want to know where the wedding will be held (an intimate inn or huge mansion with vaulted ceilings?), the level of formality, and time of day. A good florist will also ask to see the wedding dress and veil and attendants' dresses, or at least pictures and fabric swatches.

Most brides order a bouquet, flowers for the bridesmaids and flower girl (or ring bearer), boutonnieres for the groom and ushers, centerpieces for the reception, and corsages or boutonnieres for both sets of parents. You may also wish to order flowers for the ceremony or reception site and floral arrangements for pews and the rehearsal dinner.

Roses are the number-one choice of brides (followed by orchids), but pick your pleasure. While white flowers with a touch of greenery have traditionally been used for wedding bouquets, more colorful flowers are often chosen to coordinate with bridesmaid attire or wedding colors.

Keep in mind that the floral bill for a wedding date near a major flower-giving holiday like Mother's Day, Easter, or Valentine's Day will invariably be higher than at other times of the year when flowers aren't in peak demand. Florists are charged more for their flowers by wholesalers and then pass along the seasonal increases to you.

When drawing up a contract with the florist, be sure it specifies exactly what will be ordered (three bouquets, four boutonnieres, and so on), the number and kind of stems per item, and the cost *per item.* Specify where the flowers should be delivered and when. Some florists charge extra for showing up before the wedding to pin on corsages and make sure all the flowers are in place, misted with water, and arranged properly.

FABULOUS FLORAL FAKES

Artificial flowers have come a long way since the days of garish, stiff petals and stems that look anything but natural. High-quality silk flowers and greens are now available that seem just picked from the garden. There are even scent crystals and pellets on the market that add whiffs of natural floral fragrance.

For her daughter's wedding, Diane James, a floral designer based in Darien, Connecticut, created baskets, centerpieces, and sconce decorations from cascading ivy, pastel peonies, viburnum, and snapdragons. When a photographer from *Victoria* magazine came to shoot the blooms, he walked right

135

past the silk flowers, assuming they were fresh, and asked James where she'd put the silk ones. (Actually the word *silk* is used generically here; some artificial flowers are made of silk, others from latex or polyester.)

There are many advantages to using silk flowers for a wedding. The flowers last long after the big day and can be used to beautify your new home. Even cascade bouquets can be "reset" to fill a vase or planter. (James suggests ordering silk bouquets for the bridesmaids and then presenting the flowers to the attendants as gifts.) Silk floral arrangements can be delivered to the reception days before the wedding, because they won't droop or die. They also won't wilt in intense summer heat and can be easily manipulated to stay put when tucked into the slats of a gazebo or wound around an elegant banister.

THE LOVELY BRIDAL BOUQUET

The choice of a wedding bouquet depends on the styling of the gown. Bouquets vary from the loose, fresh-picked-from-the garden look, to the highly stylized formal cluster. Think tone and balance. A nosegay of daisies might look out of place with a formal long gown, while a formalized floral arrangement would appear too sober against a simple peasant dress.

Find out if the florist hand-ties and hand-wires each bloom in the bouquet or inserts them into a plastic bouquet holder filled with oasis (a foam base), which can be less stable and more bulky to carry.

The bouquet size should be in proportion to the bride. Too large a bouquet will simply overpower her and clutter her beautiful dress. And keep these shapes in mind:

Cascade A large, tear-shaped arrangement in which flowers gracefully spill downward.

Nosegay Round in shape, a tightly bound cluster of small flowers; when tiny, sometimes called a posy.

Arm Bouquet A graceful crescent shape designed to be cradled in one arm.

Biedermeier Bouquet Concentric circles of flowers in different colors.

Hand-Tied Bouquet A simple cluster of long stems, tied with a ribbon.

Spray Bouquet Usually a triangular shaped cluster of flowers.

Pomander A ball of flowers suspended from the wrist by a decorative ribbon.

When ordering the bridal bouquet, decide if you want one with a breakaway section for tossing. The florist can also prepare a minibouquet for the toss, or even a dried or silk version, so that you can save your fresh flower bouquet for drying or preserving in silica.

Alternatives to the traditional bouquet include carrying a basket with flowers draped horizontally or arranged in a formal centerpiece. Or you may wish to carry a family Bible, feather plumes, or a decorative fan.

The bride's bouquet is always different from those of her bridesmaids, but it may incorporate a few of the same flowers for a complementary look. It isn't necessary for all the bridesmaids to carry identical rubber-stamped bouquets (but stick to the same shape for a harmonious look in the keepsake photographs). The bridesmaids may also wish to wear coordinating floral wreaths or headpieces. These are typically worn across the top of the head (crescent shape) or in a crown. Fresh flowers on a barrette or hair comb look pretty as long as the blooms aren't too large, which can make a woman look as if she has a huge growth on the side of her head. (For more information on headpieces, see chapter 6 on bridal attire.)

Boutonnieres

The boutonniere is traditionally worn on the left lapel, and the bridegroom wears a different flower from the ushers or his father to distinguish his role of honor. Popular choices include rose, carnation, freesia, or lily of the valley. For a holiday wedding, consider a candy cane, gingerbread man, or holiday ornament tied with small buds and greenery.

WAYS TO SAVE ON FLOWERS AND DECORATIONS

- ❀ Choose an open, airy bouquet with fewer flowers. More flowers don't necessarily make for a lush look. A good florist can help you team larger or less expensive flowers with dramatic foliage such as ivy or eucalyptus.

- ❀ Much of the cost of a wedding bouquet is for the labor involved. Choose single stems of flowers such as calla lilies or tulips in a simple, hand-tied bouquet.

- ❀ Is your heart set on pricey, rare flowers? Place one or two prominently in the bouquet, surrounded by less expensive flowers.

- ❀ Rent rather than buy accessories such as mirrors, candelabras, votive candles, vases, or tall candlesticks.

❀ Since the altar is the focal point of the ceremony, focus on those flowers instead of pew decorations. Choose altar flowers that can double at the reception. (Make sure you assign someone to transport them to the reception.)

❀ Some couples split the cost of church flowers with another couple getting married there that same day.

❀ Forget flowers! Have the attendants carry something else, like a prayer book, Bible, fan, or basket decorated with ribbons and streamers.

❀ Use tulle bows, gold lame bows, French-wired ribbon bows, or fresh-cut branches for pew decorations.

❀ Make your own hand-tied bouquet using homegrown flowers or blooms purchased from a wholesale florist.

❀ Use a single color for value and drama. A variety of different flowers in the same shade will create dimension and texture.

❀ Make a grouping of potted plants for the centerpiece.

❀ Use blossoming bulbs as centerpieces. Hyacinths and daffodils are colorful and fragrant, too.

❀ Who says centerpieces must be flowers? Get creative. Consider a glass bowl filled with real swimming goldfish or a bucket of sand with seashells strewn around the table. Pile bowls high with beautiful lemons, oranges, bunches of grapes, or an assortment of perfect red apples. Flickering votive candles on a round or square mirror look dramatic for an evening wedding.

❀ Invest in high-quality silk floral arrangements, and use them later in your new home.

❀ Don't schedule the wedding near a major flower-giving holiday, when flower prices skyrocket.

❀ Do schedule it near the Christmas/New Year's holiday, when most sites will already be decorated with poinsettias and evergreens.

❀ For an inexpensive and undulating look, alternate tall and short centerpieces on the reception tables. Shorter flowers are often less expensive.

WEDDING FLOWER CHOICES

Flowers may be chosen for a number of characteristics.

Color

Tulips	Ranunculus
Pansies	Anemones
Mums	Daffodils
Gerbera daisies	Bachelor buttons
Lupins	Stargazer lilies with red center
Irises	

Height

Decorative branches	Gladioli
Pussy willow	Snapdragons
Zinnias	Eucalyptus branches
Larkspur	Delphinium
Long-stemmed roses	Day Lilies
Wildflowers	

Fragrance

Gardenias
Stephanotis
Freesias
Roses
Narcissus
Tuberose
Apple blossoms

Sweet William
Plumeria
Orange blossoms
Lilacs
Magnolia
Hyacinths

Low Cost

Mums
Carnations
Sweet William
Queen Anne's lace

Daisies
Baby's breath
Zinnias

Classic White "Bridal" Flowers

Gardenias
White roses
Jasmine
Dendrobium orchids
White poinsettia

Orange blossoms
Apple blossoms
Stephanotis
Camellias

Traditional, Special Meanings

Amaryllis: Pride
Apple blossom: Hope, good fortune
Blue violet: Modesty, faithfulness
Bluebells: Constancy
Blue periwinkle: Friendship
Bellflower: Gratitude
Larkspur: Laughter
Lily: Majesty

Camellia: Loveliness
Carnation: Distinction
Daisy: Innocence
Forget-me-not: Remembrance
Honeysuckle: Devoted affection
Ivy: Fidelity
Red chrysanthemum: Love
Red rose: Passion

Marigold: Affection
Mimosa: Secret love
Myrtle: Love and remembrance
Orchid: Rare beauty
Orange blossom: Purity or fertility
Peony: Bashfulness

Red tulip: Declaration of love
Rosemary: Remembrance
Violet: Modesty
White rose: Worthiness
Wood sorrel: Maternal love
Yellow tulip: Hopeless love

Herbs add fragrance to a bouquet or floral arrangement and carry special meanings too.

Herbs

Bay Laurel: Glory
Parsley: Beginnings
Rosemary: Love

Sage: Immortality
Thyme: Courage, activity

"Is there a difference between young and old love? Intensity only. We grow into companions. Love, marriage, friend, companion . . . tears, laughter, good times, bad times . . . family . . . and finally the icing on the cake: grandchildren. With marriage, there is no loneliness. You always have your best friend with you at all times."

—Doris Shulman, Connecticut July bride, on the occasion of her 50th wedding anniversary

THE WEDDING FLOWER CHECKLIST

What Will We Need?

Bouquets

Bride ☐
Maid/Matron of Honor ☐
Bridesmaids ☐
Flower girls ☐
Bride's breakaway bouquet ☐
    or separate bouquet to toss

Floral Hair Ornaments
(wreath? crescent? barrette? combs?)

Bride ☐
Maid/Matron of Honor ☐
Bridesmaids ☐
Flower girls ☐
Junior bridesmaid ☐

Boutonnieres

Bridegroom ☐
Best man ☐
Usher ☐
Father of bride ☐
Father of groom ☐

For Mothers

Corsage or wrist corsage ☐
Purse decoration flowers ☐
Arm bouquet ☐

Miscellaneous

Cake-topper flowers ☐
Flowers for garnishing ☐
    platters

Ceremony

Altar ☐
Chuppah ☐
Pews ☐
Main entrance ☐
Runner ☐

Reception

Centerpieces ☐
Head table ☐
Rest rooms ☐
Staircase railing ☐
Buffet tables ☐
Cake table ☐
Mantel ☐
Place-card table ☐

Thank-You Arrangements

Parents ☐
Honored guests ☐
Bridal consultant ☐
Officiant ☐
Out-of-town guests ☐

143

Other Considerations

Balloon arch	❑	Lighting	❑
Helium balloons anchored in bags of marbles	❑	Tent decorations	❑
		Silk flowers	❑
Rental plants	❑	Candles	❑
Fabric swags	❑	Flower boxes	❑

Chapter Nine

Photography and Videography

Of all the wedding professionals who'll help to create
your wedding memories, the photographer and videographer
will help you preserve them.

It's easy to forget that a wedding is a one-day affair. Long after the guests have

gone home and the gown has been boxed for storage, a keepsake album or video

will be a visual document of the day and a gift to future generations, too.

Weddings are the ultimate family reunion—and union. Two families gather together to witness the couple form a new family bond. Don't miss the opportunity to record these moments; there are few times in life when all your loved ones will gather for such a joyous reason.

If budget allows, try to hire both a photographer and videographer.

Videotapes may not look good hanging on a wall, says videographer Earle Greenberg of Northbrook, Illinois, but having a video means you don't have to rely on memory as you get older. He tells people, "This is the beginning of your legacy, your life together," and reminds them that the video isn't just for them, but more for their children and grandchildren.

Try to hire a photographer or videographer at least six months in advance, since the best are often booked months ahead. Sure, your Uncle Albert or college roommate can probably point a camera or camcorder and shoot, but at such an important time, why risk fuzzy pictures or images with everybody's heads cut off? And remember, too, that even camera-savvy guests will want to be part of the party that day, without the responsibility of recording the event for posterity.

PHOTOGRAPHY

A talented photographer is both artist and technician. Wedding photography is a specialized field—the photographer must be able to capture once-in-a-lifetime moments quickly (the bride tossing the bouquet or gliding down the aisle) and do it without interrupting the flow of the ceremony or the party.

Give careful consideration to the style of wedding photography you favor. The two most prevalent styles are the traditional portraiture approach and the candid, photojournalistic approach. Some photographers also concentrate on soft focus and natural-light shots.

Classic Portraiture

Will you be more comfortable following the lead of a traditional wedding photographer who will direct the action and tell you how to pose? With the portraiture approach, the photographer shoots standard composed poses that are frankly staged. He or she will tell you when and where to stand, where to look, and how to smile. The photographer might choose to do some of the portraits in a studio (as was done in the days of clunky, stationary cameras) or add special glamour effects like halos, sunbursts, and backgrounds.

Classic poses include the bride and groom staring at the ring, the bride gazing at her bouquet, and the newlyweds looking off into the distance or into each other's eyes.

While some critics groan that the classic approach is hokey and sentimental, others note that brides have been requesting these keepsake shots for decades. The shots may be formal and formulaic, but it's a formula that's been working for a long time.

Photojournalism

Over the past decade, a new breed of wedding photographers have popularized the candid wedding photojournalism approach, where the images captured for a wedding album are unrehearsed, realistic, and faithful to all the events that unfold throughout the day. Forget cookie-cutter albums: Every wedding is a personal story, so no two wedding albums should look even remotely similar.

Photojournalism is actually nothing new—newspaper, magazine, and fine-arts photographers have been snapping on-the-spot pictures for more than a century. It used to be that only celebrities and socialites could afford photojournalists to "cover" their weddings, but these days more and more photojournalists are doing mainstream weddings. Since a larger number of pictures are generally taken, the cost is sometimes higher than with a traditional portrait photographer.

Some photojournalists strive for offbeat or humorous shots, like the bride kissing her golden retriever or naughty toddlers licking the frosting off the wedding cake. Others choose to document ordinary events in an unusual way. Instead of lining up the bridesmaids for a "pretty maids in a row" shot, the photojournalist might capture them all peeking through the bride's veil.

"We do portraits and also shoot many candids," says New York City wedding photographer Wendy Stewart, who works as a team with her husband, Joel Greenberg. "During the toast I can zoom in on the person making the toast, then go wide angle and get people's reaction to the toast. Joel and I do a kind of storytelling."

Candids can happen anytime, she says, like the bride giving last-minute instructions to the flower girl before going down the aisle. "There's enough love and warmth at a wedding that you don't have to fake poses," Stewart says.

Soft-Focus Photography

This photographic style has a soft, dreamy look created by placing a filter on the camera lens.

Natural-Light Photography

A photographer using this style does not use a flash to take pictures but rather "paints" with light, not unlike paintings created by the old Dutch masters, notes photographer Gregory Geiger of Orange, Connecticut. Dark backgrounds set the subject off in bright light. This is a technically demanding style, since each image must be posed, and it demands a degree of artistry from the photographer. But when done well, the photos resemble classic artworks.

The Right Shot for the Job

To find a photographer, ask recently married friends for recommendations or call the Professional Photographers of America, a national association based in

149

Atlanta, for a list of professional photographers in your city (see appendix).

Set up an interview to meet the photographer in person and view the work firsthand. When viewing a sample book or portfolio, find out whether the work was produced by the same photographer who'll shoot your wedding, or whether it is a sample album purchased from a photo lab.

Are the shots varied and original, and do they tell a personal story? Or does it seem like you've seen it all before, just with different newlyweds? Ask to see an entire album from one wedding, rather than a compilation of best client shots. Is the composition of each photograph pleasing and balanced? Are the photos clear and in focus? Ask how the photographer will be attired at the wedding. You want someone who will remain unobtrusive and look presentable. Some go so far as to don a tuxedo in order to be dressed appropriately for such an occasion.

Album Trends

- Black-and-white photography for a dreamy, nostalgic look.
- Photos tinted with pastel colors.
- Albums combining both candids and portraits.
- Background matting in different shapes and sizes.
- Multiple images on each page of varying sizes, rather than one photo per page.
- Albums including unusual mementos—lace from the bride's wedding gown, a copy of the wedding program or invitation, or dried petals from the bride's bouquet and bridegroom's boutonniere.

When considering black-and-white photography, find out if the photographer uses one camera featuring separate film magazines loaded in both black-and-white and color (so that he or she can alternate). Some photographers use separate cameras for black-and-white and color shots, which means possibly missing a shot to put down one camera and pick up the other. The least desirable alternative is shooting with color film and printing it in black-and-white, which can produce a grainy, fuzzy image.

Certain photographers welcome a schedule of wedding events and being introduced to the key people you want photographed, like your grandmother or a college buddy. Give them the chance to do this.

Decide early when and where you want the photographs to be taken. It's less harried to do the standard portraits before the ceremony begins, but some couples still observe the old tradition about not seeing each other before the wedding.

Pictures taken following the ceremony will move along smoothly only with the cooperation of the wedding party, parents, and anyone else to be photographed. Make sure everyone knows exactly when and where to meet (and assign a trusted friend to keep them from wandering away while somebody else's shot is being done). Remember, guests wait patiently for the wedding party to emerge after the photo session, so don't hold up the whole reception because the photo-taking drags on.

Find out how many proofs will be available for preview. A good rule of thumb is to examine twice as many proofs as there are guests. If your wedding list has a hundred guests, view at least two hundred proofs before selecting the cream of the crop for the album.

One can often save money by comparing hourly fees with package prices; purchase only those services you really want. It may be less expensive to have the formal portrait shot at the reception. Or hire a professional photographer only for the ceremony and have friends take photos at the reception.

A final word about cameras. Ask the photographer whether he uses a 35 mm camera or a "medium format" system. The medium format camera produces larger negatives (2 $^1/_4$ inches square) than the 35 mm, which in turn makes it easier to crop and enlarge, without grainy results. The 2 $^1/_4$ inch negatives are popular because they lend themselves more easily to retouching, for people who want to amend wrinkles or blemishes, photographer Wendy Stewart says. But 35 mm is often preferable for candids. When Stewart and her husband shoot a wedding, clients get the best of both worlds: she uses a medium-format camera, while he shoots with 35 mm.

"I tell people that photography and videography are an investment, not an expense. We document the event like nobody else can. And with all the money you spend on the event, afterward the flowers are gone, the ice sculpture is gone, the food is gone, and if the photography and videography don't capture and record that stuff, you are not going to remember all those beautiful things."

—Videographer Michael Carter, MBC Video, Redmond, Washington

Get It in Writing

Make sure the contract includes a detailed cost estimate of specific coverage (number of posed/candid shots and number of proofs for review), the schedule, and the photographer's cancellation policy. For instance, what happens if you cancel before the photographer has time to arrange for an alternate date? Does he keep the deposit even if he rebooks?

Include the length of time negatives will be held and how long prices will be in effect after the wedding. Do the bride and groom get to keep the negatives? Find out if all reprints must be ordered at the same time in one batch. That is, does the photographer expect you to consolidate your mother's and sister's photo choices with your own for a single list?

Some photographers refuse to release photographs until everyone involved in the wedding has paid for their orders. Which means if your maid of honor ordered prints but still hasn't paid for them two months later, the photographer may hold up your album until the matter is settled.

The contract should also include delivery times and specific details about rights of ownership and reproduction. Often, the photographer remains the owner of all negatives taken at the wedding but must get your consent before reproducing any pictures for publication. If you don't want your wedding pictures included in the photographer's portfolio (shown as samples to other clients), it's important to stipulate that up front.

Great Photography Ideas

- ❀ Arrange for a group portrait of all the wedding guests at the reception, or outside the ceremony site.

- ❀ Place disposable cameras on every table at the reception and let guests capture every moment for you! (Be sure to make clear whether the cameras are intended as take-home party favors or

153

whether you expect them to be left behind for processing.)

❀ Arrange for the photographer (or a friend) to take a photograph of every guest/couple to enclose with thank-you notes after the wedding. For a themed wedding, include appropriate props like half-masks, feather boas, or unusual hats.

❀ Assign a close friend or loved one to help the photographer identify special people to photograph—Grandpa, your favorite niece—or especially sensitive situations. ("My divorced mother would prefer not to have keepsake shots of Dad's new girlfriend.")

❀ Take extra pictures of the children at the wedding (guests or wedding-party members) to present as holiday or birthday gifts to their parents later in the year.

❀ Turn the tables on your guests! Have the photographer or an assistant turn the camera on the guests to capture their reactions to the cake-cutting or the walk down the aisle.

❀ Ask the photographer to shoot a portrait of the bride and groom with the youngest and oldest guests at the wedding.

Questions to Ask the Photographer

❀ Will the photographer I've chosen be the one who will shoot my wedding?

❀ How many rolls of film do you typically shoot? What brand of film and paper do you use?

- Do you shoot black-and-white using film for black-and-white prints, or do you shoot in color and then print in black-and-white?

- What kind of camera do you use? Medium format or 35 mm?

- Can your camera accommodate different film magazines so that you can switch back and forth from color to black-and-white, and vice versa?

- How long have you been doing this? Do you shoot mainly weddings? If not, where else do you work as a photographer (art studio, newspaper, magazine, corporation)?

- What packages or levels of service do you offer?

- Do you have a backup in case of illness or an emergency?

- What is your philosophy of wedding photography? Do you prefer to shoot mostly candids . . . classic portraiture . . . soft focus?

- Are you a member of any professional organizations?

- Will you follow a list of suggested shots?

- How long after the wedding can we expect to view the proofs (some photographers call them "previews")? When can we expect the finished album?

- What kind of retouching can you do ("opening" closed eyes, or "removing" teeth braces, wrinkles, blemishes, and so on)?

- What kind of albums do you use, and what are they made of (leather, plastic, cardboard)? Are the pages acid-free (for longer life), and do the mats come in different shapes and colors?

155

"We had two videographers shooting our wedding: one was at the altar and the other was at the back of the church. The videographer at the altar took reactions of the audience during the ceremony, and the videographer at the back of the church took the processional and standard views of the entire church."

—Tref Lowe, Indiana August bride

VIDEOGRAPHY

Many couples want a video record of their wedding. It captures all the spontaneous movement, noise and excitement, and emotion. The cost for a video package varies regionally, but expect to spend at least $350 to several thousand dollars.

Fees depend upon the number of cameras used, the quality of the equipment, the amount of postproduction editing, and time spent by the videographer(s) at the wedding. The advantage of two cameras is that one videographer can be shooting from the back, while the other shoots the events from the altar or balcony. The two views can later be merged for a complete perspective.

If cost is a factor, hire a professional videographer for a limited number of hours to capture the most important moments, and supplement that tape with home videos made by talented friends.

Be forewarned: Many houses of worship place restrictions on the use of photo and video equipment, so check with the officiant first. A professional will know how to make accommodations, such as using a powerful zoom lens to shoot through a crack in a door or from a balcony or window.

Shop wisely, since there's nothing worse than a professional video that looks like a home movie. View demonstration tapes and look carefully at the details:

- ❀ Does the video capture all the major events of the wedding but still include spontaneous shots and personal vignettes?

- ❀ Does the lighting look natural, or are the people bathed in blinding, garish spotlights?

- ❀ Was the camera held steady?

- ❀ Is the color sharp and the sound clear?

- ❀ Are voices audible, or is there a lot of background rumble?

- ❀ Does the video look seamless as it fades from one shot to the next? Does the videographer allow time for relationships and stories to develop before moving to another subject?

Editing is all important to a well-produced video. Ask whether the editing will be done in a postproduction studio or within the camera (that is, by turning the camera on and off). Most videographers will shoot everything through the entire ceremony and reception, although the finished tape is edited to one or two hours long. Some will also provide you with a "highlights" tape fifteen to twenty minutes long.

Videography is a relatively new field, but the technology changes all the time. Ask what kind of training the videographer has received, how many weddings he or she has done, and whether the equipment can handle low-light conditions, such as candlelight or a sanctuary that prohibits extra lighting. Some videographers now use the "bounce" lighting technique in which light is bounced off the ceiling to produce a reflection that illuminates subjects without harsh glare. Experts recommend that videos be shot in a Hi 8 or Super VHS format to maintain high quality after editing.

Video Trends and Techniques

- ❁ Adding prewedding stories and interview segments
- ❁ Baby pictures of the couple incorporated into the videotape
- ❁ Superimposed music and graphics
- ❁ A separate wedding-highlights tape
- ❁ Special effects such as animation or the addition of dates and titles
- ❁ Cordless microphones worn by bride and groom to record the wedding vows and toast.

Chapter Ten

Invitations and Accessories

Set the date? Now spread the word!

Wedding invitations make a first and truly lasting impression. As the first official announcement of your wedding date, the invitation reflects the style and formality of your wedding and becomes a memento.

Choosing wedding stationery means more than selecting invitations. There are lots of decisions to make: paper color and stock, ink color, lettering style, printing process, and whether to choose liners and envelopes and all kinds of little extras. At the same time as ordering invitations, you may wish to order thank-you notes, personal stationery, at-home cards, reception cards, or wedding announcements.

Sound confusing? It needn't be.

Begin by choosing a supplier who is knowledgeable about wording, type styles, and papers. Wedding stationery may be ordered through a bridal consultant, in a bridal shop, stationery or jewelry store, department store, or through mail-order catalogues.

Generally, whoever hosts the wedding issues the invitations. Traditionally, that meant the bride's parents. But today, the nearest living relative, an important loved one, or the bride and groom themselves may send them out.

WHEN TO ORDER

Invitations should be selected as soon as the date is set and the guest list is complete, at least three to six months in advance to allow time for ordering, proofreading the text, and addressing the invitations yourself or hiring a calligrapher.

Invitations should be mailed four to six weeks before a wedding (and up to eight weeks ahead for a summer or holiday wedding, when guests often have competing social obligations).

Expect to spend anywhere from around $40 to $1,000 for a hundred invitations. Custom and handcrafted designs are the priciest.

MAKING THE LIST

Regardless of who is paying for the wedding, the guest list is usually compiled from several sources: the bride's friends and co-workers, the groom's friends and co-workers, the bride's relatives, the groom's relatives, and any friends or colleagues the couple share in common. (*Her* people, *his* people, and *their* people.)

It's customary to send invitations to each member of the wedding party as well as the officiant and all guests over the age of sixteen. If the officiant is married, include his or her spouse. To calculate the number to order, figure one for each couple, plus one for each single guest and another for his or her date. (Don't feel obliged to include dates. But if you do, they should receive a separate invitation.)

Include a few extras to keep in a family album as mementos or to frame and display. It's important to order more invitations than you expect to need: there may be last-minute invitees, and many companies charge an extra setup fee or have a 25- or 50-invitation minimum for reorders. Be sure to order extra envelopes (in case of goofs while addressing them).

161

GUEST LIST WARS

Is the guest list out of control? Pare it down, rather than assuming a certain percentage of no-shows! Couples often make the mistake of depending on some guests not making it. *Don't count on it!* There's nothing worse than getting anxious every time another guest says yes because you didn't know when to say no.

According to advice columnist Ann Landers, the wedding guest list can become "the battlefield on which parents on both sides fight the bitterest wars." Countless family relationships, she observes, have been seriously damaged because of it.

In her *Guide for Brides,* Landers notes that since the bride's parents usually pay for the wedding, they have the right to tell the groom's family how many guests they may invite. If the bride's family is much larger than the groom's, a disproportionate number of invitations should go to her family. Yet if the reverse is true, the groom's family should be allotted more invitations, even if the bride's family is paying for the wedding. It isn't always even-steven.

Some people prepare a "must invite" and "want to invite" list. Invitations for the "must" list are sent out, and if there are regrets from that list, invitations from the "want" list are mailed. (But never send an invitation less than three weeks ahead, or you'll insult the guest.)

Catholic couples may arrange with their local diocese to send a copy of their wedding invitation to the Pope. A papal blessing marking the sacred occasion (marriage is considered a sacrament) will be sent in return. Keep in mind that to get this blessing will incur a minimal cost and will have to be done long in advance. If you send a copy to the President of the United States in Washington, DC, you'll receive an acknowledgment signed by the President and First Lady.

CHOICES AND MORE CHOICES

Today's brides can choose from a staggering array of colored inks, scripts, and papers in different shapes and sizes—round, geometric, oversize, you name it. Luxurious details now include moiré bows, hand-painted flowers, watercolor effects, laser-cut designs, shimmery embossed designs, colored liners and borders, and even envelopes dripping with lace, pearl sprays, or netting.

With all the choices available, it's possible to coordinate the wedding stationery with the wedding theme or the color of the attendants' gowns. Invitations are available with western themes, holiday themes, and religious symbols, as well as traditional African-American accents like kente-cloth-inspired borders and traditional tribal symbols.

Contemporary invitations and handwritten or verbal invitations are fine for a small or informal wedding. A formal or semiformal wedding, however, calls for the traditional wedding invitation.

The standard traditional invitation has a left-side fold, black ink, and double envelope, and it is printed on ivory or ecru paper. The type is set by engraving or thermography.

Engraving is a centuries-old printing process where the paper is pressed onto an etched metal plate, creating letters that are slightly raised on the paper. Engraving is elegant but also costly and time-consuming, since a plate must be custom engraved for each client.

Thermography, a less expensive alternative, is a process in which ink and powder are fused together on the paper to create a raised-lettering effect. The average person really can't tell the difference between engraving and thermography.

163

Don't assume thermographed invitations are invariably cheaper: the total stationery cost comprises the number of invitations ordered, the paper quality, and any special trims, liners, or envelopes.

Offset or Laser Printing are both inexpensive forms of printing (done on a press or using a laser printer) where the ink lies flat on the paper. Although the look is attractive, these processes are appropriate mainly for casual or informal invitations.

Home Computer Printing Many personal computers now have software programs for printing invitations for weddings and parties. These are super for informal invitations, and the price is certainly right. With these, it's easy to add frills, borders, and graphics and to use elegant fonts.

Handwritten Invitations For an informal wedding, buy beautiful invitations at a stationer and write them yourself using a fine-tip pen with black ink.

Computerized or Handwritten Calligraphy is an elegant form of script featuring flourishes and curls. The look can be achieved by computer (available now in most stationery stores) or done by hand.

A calligrapher usually creates a master copy for the wedding invitation, which is then replicated by engraving, thermography, or offset printing. Unless the wedding has a handful of guests, it would be far too costly for a calligrapher to write every single invitation by hand. Place cards and outside envelopes, however, are usually done individually by hand.

When choosing a calligrapher, ask to see samples of the work. The calligrapher will want to know specific details like whether you want the number seven crossed or not, how you would like the letters Z and Y to be written, and whether you prefer a plain script or a fancy one with serifs (elaborate curls and flourishes). As a kindness to guests, choose serifs that are easy to read.

PAPER AND MORE PAPER

Wedding invitations come with an outer envelope and inner envelope, as well as delicate tissue paper. The invitation itself is placed fold-side down in the unsealed inner envelope, along with all enclosures. Then the inside envelope is placed into the larger outer envelope (face side up toward the flap) for addressing and mailing.

The tradition of inserting tissue paper between the wedding invitation and envelope came about when a printer in a hurry used tissue paper as a blotter, instead of waiting for the ink to dry naturally. It's now considered an elegant and sophisticated way to go.

In addition to the invitation, consider possible enclosures.

Response Card When returned by guests, these give you an accurate head count. As a courtesy to guests, enclose stamped, self-addressed envelopes with the response cards for easy mailing.

Some couples omit the response card and prefer their guests to write a formal handwritten note, along the lines of "Mr. and Mrs. Mark Hampton accept with pleasure (or regret that they are unable to accept) your kind invitation for Sunday, the fourth of March." The note should be written on white stationery in blue or black ink, paralleling the wording on the invitation.

Reception Card States the time, date and place of the reception. Used to invite guests to the reception following the ceremony, it need not be mailed back.

The Ceremony Card Used when everyone is invited to the reception but only a select few are invited to the ceremony.

Pew Cards Necessary only for society, royal, or very large, fancy weddings, this indicates seating assignment at the ceremony and should be presented for admittance.

165

You may also choose to order thank-you notes, informal cards (folded notes printed with your married name or monogram on front), and at-home cards, to inform friends of your new address. Maps and directions to the reception and ceremony are a thoughtful touch. Out-of-town guests who'll be spending a few days in town for the wedding will appreciate a list of local restaurants, shopping centers, and points of interest.

WEDDING ANNOUNCEMENTS

Often, there are people you'll want to notify of your wedding but don't feel inclined to invite for any number of reasons—they might live too far away or be casual acquaintances. In this case, a wedding announcement will do. Wedding announcements are *never* sent before the wedding date. The announcement includes the wedding date but not the location, and therefore is not an invitation to attend.

People who receive wedding announcements are not obligated to send a wedding gift. (While we're on the subject, a wedding invitation doesn't necessarily obligate a guest to send a gift either. If a guest does *not* attend the wedding, no gift is required.)

The Word on Wording

Etiquette books devote entire chapters to the subject of wording the invitations! Consult the enclosed sidebar for specific cases, but in general, keep these points in mind:

- ❀ Full names are used (not nicknames or abbreviations), and dates, times, and addresses are spelled out.

- ❀ Each line of the wedding invitation is centered, for a balanced look.

- ❀ Traditional British spelling is often used for the words *honour* and *favour*.

- ❀ Courtesy titles (Mr., Miss, Ms., Mrs.) are used. When appropriate, professional titles should be used. Doctor may be abbreviated as Dr. A priest or minister is called The Reverend (note use of "The"), and a judge is called The Honorable. Rabbi, however, doesn't need the "The" (thus, Rabbi Ehrenkrantz, The Reverend Miller).

- ❀ Military titles are handled by rank. According to *Modern Bride* magazine, enlisted people and noncommissioned officers may include their branch of the service underneath their name. Titles for officers (above captain in the army and lieutenant senior grade in the navy) precede their name, and the branch of service appears on the line below. *Modern Bride* notes that the names of junior officers should be placed on the first line, with title and branch of service on the next line.

Double-check the spelling and wording of the invitation and request a proofread before the invitations are printed. To be on the safe side, ask a friend to proofread it too—letter by letter, and line by line.

Don't forget to weigh the entire invitation packet to determine correct postage.

167

SAMPLE INVITATION WORDING

When the bride's parents host the wedding:

Mr. and Mrs. George Lawlor

request the honour of your presence

at the marriage of their daughter

Margaret Beth

to

Mr. Peter Arthur Flagg

on Saturday, the third of March

nineteen hundred and ninety-six

at three o'clock in the afternoon

St. Maurice Church

100 Glenbrook Road

Indianapolis, Indiana

If one parent is deceased, and mother is not remarried:

Mrs. George Lawlor

requests the honour of your presence

at the marriage of her daughter

Margaret Beth

to

Mr. Peter Arthur Flagg

Father not remarried:

Mr. George Lawlor
requests the honour of your presence
at the marriage of his daughter
Margaret Beth
to
Mr. Peter Arthur Flagg

Mother remarried:

Mr. and Mrs. Mark Cross
request the honour of your presence
at the marriage of her daughter
Margaret Beth Lawlor
to
Mr. Peter Arthur Flagg

Father remarried:

Mr. and Mrs. George Lawlor
request the honour of your presence
at the marriage of his daughter
Margaret Beth
to
Mr. Peter Arthur Flagg

(Note: There is no need to add Margaret Beth's last name, since it's the same as her father's.)

169

If both parents are deceased, a close relative or friend may issue the invitation:

Mr. and Mrs. James Stevens
request the honour of your presence
at the marriage of her sister
Margaret Beth Lawlor
to
Mr. Peter Arthur Flagg

. . . or the bride and groom may host their own wedding:

Miss Margaret Beth Lawlor
and
Mr. Peter Arthur Flagg
request the honour of your presence
at their marriage

If the bride's parents are divorced . . .

I.   Divorced mother issuing invitation (if she has not remarried, she may use her maiden name and her married name):

Mrs. Martha Grimes Lawlor
requests the honour of your presence
at the marriage of her daughter
Margaret Beth
to
Mr. Peter Arthur Flagg

2. Divorced father issuing invitation:

Mr. George Lawlor

requests the honour of your presence

at the marriage of his daughter

Margaret Beth

to

Mr. Peter Arthur Flagg

3. Divorced parents both issuing invitation:

Mrs. Martha Lawlor

and

Mr. George Lawlor

request the honour of your presence

at the marriage of their daughter

When both the bride's and bridegroom's parents issue the invitation together:

Mr. and Mrs. George Lawlor

and

Mr. and Mrs. James Flagg

request the honour of your presence

at the marriage of their children

Margaret Beth

and

Peter Arthur

(Note: There is no need to include the children's last names.)

When the groom's family hosts the wedding:

Mr. and Mrs. James Flagg

request the honour of your presence

at the marriage of

Miss Margaret Beth Lawlor

to their son

Mr. Peter Arthur Flagg

When the invitation is for a second wedding:

Mr. and Mrs. George Lawlor

request the honour of your presence

at the marriage of their daughter

Ms. Margaret Beth Tatton

to

Mr. Peter Arthur Flagg

When the ceremony is private and the invitation is to the reception only:

Mr. and Mrs. George Lawlor

request the pleasure of your company

at the wedding reception of their daughter

Margaret Beth

and

Mr. Peter Arthur Flagg

Saturday, the third of March

nineteen hundred and ninety-six

at 5 o'clock in the afternoon

Greenbriar Country Club

12 Poplar Avenue

Indianapolis, Indiana

In the case of a double wedding, the invitation wording depends on the relationship between the brides. If the brides are sisters:

Mr. and Mrs. George Lawlor

request the honour of your presence

at the marriage of their daughters

Margaret Beth

to

Mr. Peter Arthur Flagg

and

Anne Marie

to

Mr. Edward Wood

If the brides are not sisters, the oldest bride goes first, and the parents of both brides are included:

Mr. and Mrs. George Lawlor

and

Mr. and Mrs. James Damon

request the honour of your presence

at the marriage of their daughters

Margaret Beth Lawlor

to

Mr. Peter Arthur Flagg

and

Joanne Suzanne Damon

to

Mr. Henry Cleaver

In the case of military titles, follow these guidelines. Let's say Margaret Beth Lawlor is marrying a petty officer or seaman; it would read:

Mr. and Mrs. George Lawlor

request the honour of your presence

at the marriage of their daughter

Margaret Beth

to

Peter Arthur Flagg

United States Navy

If the future groom is a navy ensign or higher rank:

Margaret Beth

to

Peter Arthur Flagg

Ensign, United States Navy

If the future groom is in the marine corps, army, or air force and is a noncommissioned officer or private:

Margaret Beth

to

Peter Arthur Flagg

United States Army

for a lieutenant:

Margaret Beth

to

Peter Arthur Flagg

Lieutenant, United States Army

for a captain or higher rank:

to

Captain Peter Arthur Flagg

United States Army

The wording on contemporary invitations is far less formal, and any sentiment

may be chosen. Here are some examples:

Margaret Beth Lawlor

and

Peter Arthur Flagg

Invite you to share in the joy of their marriage.

This celebration of love will be

on Saturday, the third of March

nineteen hundred and ninety-six

or

Margaret Beth Lawlor

and

Peter Arthur Flagg

will pledge their love as one

on Saturday, the third of March, etc.

175

A tremendous day in our lives

is drawing near.

We would be honored if you could share

in our joy

as we are united in marriage

on Saturday, the third of March

"The florist I went to gave me a great tip: When sending out invitations with a response card, put a number on the back of the card to correspond with the guest's name on a master list. If they forget to put their name on the response card, you can match up the name with the number on the list."

—Elizabeth Mushinsky, Connecticut September bride

ACCESSORIES

When ordering invitations, couples often give special consideration to accessories and party favors. Napkins, matchbooks, inscribed albums, ring pillows, garters, engraved goblets, and cake tops are often available through a wedding stationer, mail-order catalogue, or bridal shop. For ideas, flip through the pages of the major bridal magazines, especially the advertising sections at the back of the books featuring ads for mail-order favors.

Will party favors be included at your wedding reception? For some ethnic groups, party favors are an essential part of the reception, and guests would be offended by not going home with a small token. Favors are a thoughtful remembrance and a nice way of thanking guests for sharing in your celebration. One favor is usually given to each couple. Popular choices include

- Jordan almonds (symbolizing joy and fertility) tied up in tulle bundles
- Beribboned split of champagne
- Porcelain vase or figurine
- Candy boxes filled with Hershey "hugs" or "kisses" or chocolate truffles
- Fresh evergreen seedling for planting in celebration of the marriage
- Small potted plant
- Silverplated mirror
- Picture frame (which can double as place card)

- ❀ Silver napkin ring

- ❀ Bottles of soap bubbles for blowing

- ❀ Flower or vegetable seed packets in decorative pot

- ❀ Box of animal crackers

- ❀ For a holiday wedding: mini Christmas trees and Christmas ornaments, especially glass ornaments hand painted with the couple's names and wedding date

- ❀ Candles or decorative candlestick

- ❀ Plastic or crystal wine goblet.

Looking for a green favor that keeps on growing? The Greenworld Project, a company based in Kingston, New York, has a line of wedding favors including live tree seedlings and tree and wildflower seed packets. Live tree seedlings are also available from Celebrations in Green by Expressions, in Manchester, Pennsylvania.

Chapter Eleven

Children at the Wedding

Every family has one. An adorable little child
who'd look darling in a flouncy flower-girl dress
or velvet ring-bearer suit. Cute, huh?

Think twice before you melt. There are pros and cons to having children at a wedding—either as members of the wedding party or as guests.

While many couples consider weddings a special kind of adult party, a growing number of brides and grooms are encouraging parents to bring Junior along.

The question of whether or not to include children can be a sticky one. In some cultures, children are expected to be included, and no relatives would dream of showing up without them. After all, young children lend joy and spontaneity to a party and are mesmerized by the fantasy and pageantry of a wedding. Telling Cousin Martha to leave little Janie at home may be taken as a personal insult.

On the flip side, even well-mannered children can grow restless, noisy, or disruptive at a wedding, especially when their meals or naptimes have been interrupted. What child wouldn't get cranky after being expected to sit through a long ceremony or be "a perfect gentleman" all day? And even though kids don't eat much, reception fees are usually based on a per-person charge.

Wedding consultant Pat Bruneau loves kids but advises brides to think long and hard about including young ones in the wedding. "If at all possible, try to make it an adults' reception and make note of that on the reception card so that people know," she says. "'Adults reception immediately following the ceremony' is nice and clear. 'No Children' sounds so cold." This limitation is as much a kindness for the child as for the adults, particularly concerning a formal or ultraformal evening wedding, where children's bedtimes are certain to be ignored.

Of course, many out-of-town wedding guests have no choice but to bring their children. If the reception is in a hotel, consider hiring a baby-sitter who will stay in one room with all the children and entertain them. For a wedding in a reception hall, Bruneau once arranged for an adjacent room to be trans-formed into a kids' room, complete with baby-sitter, portable television, VCR stocked with lots of kids' tapes, and crayons, snacks, and coloring books. The children were happy and their parents were free to check on them anytime.

Including very young children in the bridal party can be risky business. There's the chance your wedding will go down in memory as the one where the flower girl got halfway down the aisle and ran back to Mommy—or worse, announced she had to go to the potty. Deciding where to draw the line is a personal choice. Some couples invite only those children in the wedding party, or just first cousins, babies who must be breastfed, kids over twelve, or only the children of siblings.

It isn't the couple's responsibility to hire a sitter for guests and fret over finding a travel crib or high chair. A thoughtful bride will provide a list of responsible sitters so parents can make the arrangements themselves.

When including children in the wedding party, how young is too young? Keep in mind the child's age, size, and maturity. Most wedding planners say the ideal range for flower girls and ring bearers is around four to eight years old. Girls eight to fourteen are often considered junior bridesmaids. Every child is different. Many look precious and sail through their wedding roles without a hitch. But bridal consultants often swap horror stories about what can go wrong.

Everyone wants their two-year-old niece as the flower girl, but realize that when a small child is standing at the start of an aisle and an entire congregation of people are standing up and looking at him or her, it's terrifying. There's the risk the child will freeze like a scared bunny and refuse to go down the aisle. Whether the child freezes or needs to be coaxed, it's not fair to anyone, including the child. And it's going to be in your video!

Including children in the wedding can be an important consideration for a second marriage, especially when you're trying to foster a sense of family unity.

Entrusting a child with a special job to do is a way of honoring him or her. But how can you include kids who are too old to be ring bearer or refuse to wear anything but cutoff jeans and sandals? Ask them what they'd *like* to do.

Most kids, especially preteens, know exactly what they want and how they'd like to be included. They may be eager to share the spotlight or they may simply dread the thought of doing *anything* in front of the whole congregation. Here are some alternative contributions they can make:

- Hand out wedding programs or directions to the reception.
- Play a musical instrument or sing a solo.
- Read a passage during the liturgy, or recite a poem.
- Serve as altar boy or altar girl.
- Greet guests.
- Sit at the head table in a place of honor.
- Turn pages for a musician.
- Carry the bride's train.
- Hand out flowers to guests or scatter rose petals.
- Follow the photographer around, pointing out special people to photograph.
- Help take care of the gifts at the reception.
- Take candid pictures of the family and bridal party.
- Carry ceremony flowers to the reception.
- Help guests find their seating assignments.
- Present wedding favors to guests.
- Help serve the wedding cake.
- Keep track of the bride's purse or emergency kit.

- Be in charge of the guest book.

- Ask guests to sign pages in a scrapbook.

TIPS FOR INCLUDING YOUNG CHILDREN IN THE WEDDING

- Keep dresses short so that the child is less apt to trip.

- Avoid scratchy slips or underskirts or downright heavy gowns.

- Make sure shoes are comfortable and have nonskid soles. (Ballerina slippers are a perennial favorite because they're soft, pretty, and inexpensive.)

- Choose hair ornaments (barrettes, bows, headbands) that won't pinch or fall off easily, or floral headpieces that are sturdy and comfortable.

- Avoid flowers that will wilt or discolor if the child tugs at them all day. A good choice is any wreath made from carnations, daisy pompoms, baby's breath, or silk flowers, because these all have strong stems.

- Take photographs of the child early in the day before boredom or fatigue sets in. Spontaneous photos of children are marvelous because they aren't self-conscious, and there's a trend for wedding photojournalists to snap candid shots of the children at intervals throughout the day. These pictures range from the flower girl helping the bride fluff her gown before

183

the wedding to shots of children playing tag in their wedding finery, or the ring bearer falling asleep on Dad's shoulder at reception's end.

- ❀ Decide whether the child will stand in the receiving line. It can be scary to smile and shake hands with strangers when you're just three or four.

- ❀ Be sure the child knows exactly where Mom and Dad will be sitting during the ceremony. Appoint an adult to tell the flower girl or ring bearer what to do and when.

- ❀ Following the processional down the aisle, the child attendant may wish to join Mom and Dad in the pews, rather than stand with the bridal party.

- ❀ Escort the child to the bathroom just before the walk down the aisle. (Mothers know what happens when young kids get nervous.)

- ❀ Never use the real wedding rings on the ring bearer's pillow. Use fake ceremonial ones, and sew them securely on.

- ❀ Consider asking a baby-sitter to pick up the child at the reception around bedtime.

- ❀ Relax and be ready for anything! If the child seems skittish about performing any duties, don't push! Remember, guests understand that kids will be kids.

Chapter Twelve

Wedding Ceremonies and Customs

With all the hoopla and pageantry of choosing a gown and planning a dream reception, it's easy to lose sight of the real reason for the big day itself—the wedding ceremony.

Of the many social rituals we observe throughout our lives, the marriage ceremony is probably the most universal and deeply rooted in history. Wedding vows are both a promise and a declaration of consent to be witnessed by others. Nearly every society in the world has its own conception of how men and women should bond, with stylized ceremonies for marking the occasion.

Many contemporary wedding ceremonies still re-create betrothal rites dating back many centuries. Even then, the ingredients were the same: a bride, a bridegroom, and a dignitary or religious elder to sanction and witness their bond in front of God and/or the community. The word *wed* actually refers to an ancient custom of purchasing a wife. The "wed" was literally the stuff (goats, chickens, gold coins, property) the groom offered in order to "buy" the bride from her father. Later this tradition gradually evolved into the concept of a dowry where the bride's parents offered money, land, or goods to the groom for marrying the bride.

WHERE TO BEGIN?

Arranging a wedding ceremony begins with a basic decision: Will it be civil or religious? Either way, the planning should begin as early as possible. You can't say, "I do!" without a venue.

Many houses of worship impose restrictions on days when ceremonies are permitted, such as no marriages performed on holy days or during certain religious festivals. Some faiths even prohibit kissing at the ceremony. And in some religions, a waiting period of six months to a year is expected because marriage is considered a serious and enduring commitment, not to be entered into lightly.

You may be required to undergo premarital counseling or marriage preparation programs that can last weeks or months. In the Catholic Church, these programs are called pre-Cana preparation. The couple is usually expected to attend a weekend "engaged encounter session" together, or weekly meetings with a parish priest.

Occasionally, it is possible to condense these requirements into a shorter time frame—if, for instance, the future bride or groom is being called up for military service or is suddenly relocated to a job in another part of the country. Check with the officiant, but don't count on it; the reason had better be pressing.

Divorce and interfaith marriage can also cause long delays, and you may not be able to marry until you meet specific requirements.

Finally, there is often a lot of paperwork involved in preparation for a marriage ceremony, which means tracking down divorce papers, citizenship papers, and birth or baptismal certificates. Allow yourself *plenty of time* for all this.

Couples are sometimes surprised to learn that if they are not practicing members of a particular church or temple, the officiant may turn down their request to marry there. Also, some congregations don't allow "guest" clergy (of their religious faith or any other) to perform weddings in their house of worship—only the "home" clergy can officiate. If you are new to the area or have your heart set on a particular church or temple, this can pose a problem. Keep calling around until you find an officiant willing to welcome you.

INTERFAITH CEREMONY

When planning an interfaith marriage, it's especially important for the partners to meet with officiants from both faiths. Think carefully about why you want an interfaith religious ceremony and how you will continue to practice your separate faiths without conflict or stress.

Many officiants will want to know how you plan to rear future children. (Will you follow your faith, his faith, or try to balance both?) Some houses of worship will allow officiants from both faiths to officiate together. This can be a rewarding celebration of unity and diversity. Or consider holding the ceremonies back to back. Say, first a Catholic ceremony, and then a Jewish ceremony.

"Interfaith weddings are taking place all across the country now, as America is made up of so many different cultures and religions," says Millie Martini Bratten, *Bride's* magazine editor-in-chief. "What an interfaith wedding can do in the most positive sense is be a forum to enlighten both sides of this new family to the best traditions of each faith and what is important about them. As an interfaith couple, you discover a lot about how different you are from one another during the wedding planning, and what is different can be frightening. It can be wonderful, too."

THE COMMON THREAD

Each religion has established standards for how a marriage ceremony proceeds, and it's impossible to do justice to every religious faith in these pages. For details about the specific content for your denomination's wedding ceremony, consult an officiant. There are often complex rules about who walks in with whom, and special prayers or procedures.

Generally, most wedding services consist of a greeting stage, selected readings or blessings, a section on intent ("Do you promise to love, honor . . ." etc.), a vows exchange, an exchange of rings, a blessing or announcement of declaration, and the processional.

Following are highlights of several religious ceremonies:

Catholic Wedding Ceremony

The Catholic faith views marriage as one of seven holy sacraments and a life-long commitment. The Catholic ceremony begins with the greeting, in which the priest welcomes the couple. The ceremony also includes the Liturgy of the Word, which shows the importance of Christian marriage in the history of salvation; the consent section, in which the priest asks the couple to declare their consent to marry; and the blessing and exchange of rings.

At least three weeks before the wedding, banns must be read. A public declaration of the intent to marry, banns are usually published in the church bulletin and read out loud each Sunday for three weeks prior to the ceremony. Couples often save the church bulletin announcing their banns as a memento.

A Catholic ceremony is not valid unless performed by a priest, in the presence of two Catholic witnesses. The most religious Catholic ceremony is the Nuptial Mass, which often takes place at noon. This includes a full mass and Holy Communion, in addition to the exchange of wedding vows.

Jewish Wedding Ceremony

The Jewish marriage ceremony may be performed on all days except the Sabbath, fast days, and Jewish holidays. It need not take place in a synagogue to be valid.

The couple's parents may take part in the processional, and the bride and bridegroom join the rabbi under the chuppah, or marriage canopy, during the ceremony. The chuppah (sometimes spelled "huppah") is a symbol of both the tents of nomadic ancestors and the new Jewish family that forms beneath it during the wedding ceremony.

The marriage ceremony differs among the three main groups within the Jewish religion: Orthodox, Conservative, and Reform—so it's best to check with your rabbi for specific requirements. In general, most Jewish ceremonies include the presentation of the *ketubah*, or marriage document, by the groom. This document outlines the groom's responsibilities to his future wife. The signing of the *ketubah* by the groom and witnesses is an important highlight.

At both Orthodox and Conservative ceremonies, the groom and all other men cover their heads with caps or yarmulkes, and the bride's head is covered with a veil. And for both groups, the ring is placed on the forefinger of the bride's right hand. At a Reform ceremony, however, the ring goes on the fourth finger of the bride's left hand.

The "seven blessings" read by the rabbi are the essence of a Jewish wedding. These include the prayer over the wine, praise for God for having created the universe, a prayer for God to bless the couple with children, and a call for the groom to rejoice with his bride.

One of the best-known customs of the Jewish wedding is the breaking of the glass, which signifies the fragility of love and is a reminder of the ancient destruction of the Holy Temple—as well as the fact that life brings both joy and sorrow. Another, more obscure custom is the *badekan* (veiling) ceremony, in which the groom sees the bride before the wedding to confirm her identity—a tradition that evolved from the Biblical story of Jacob, who was in love with Rachel but was tricked into marrying her older sister, Leah, who was disguised by a veil.

Protestant Wedding Ceremony

Many Protestant ceremonies begin with the well-known "Dearly beloved, we are gathered together" speech. Marriage is considered a binding and serious union, but not a sacrament, and many ministers are willing to perform the wedding ceremony outside the house of worship, making it possible to have the ceremony and reception at the same site.

The Protestant ceremony features vows that are familiar to most people, along the lines of "I Charles, take you, Diana, to have and to hold from this day forward, for better, for worse; for richer, for poorer; in sickness and in health; to love and to cherish, until death do us part."

The specific ceremony differs among Protestant denominations, which include Lutheran, Baptist, Methodist, Presbyterian, and many others. Some require premarital counseling or meetings with the officiant and serious religious preparation beforehand. It's not possible to do justice to them all here.

Did You Know . . . ?

In the Mormon faith, only couples of great faith and "worthiness" may be married in a "sealing" ceremony for eternity. Mormon civil ceremonies may also be performed, in which a couple are considered married until death do them part.

For a marriage to be valid in the Episcopal church, it must include a declaration of "free and unfettered consent" and an exchange of solemn vows.

In the traditional Quaker ceremony, the groom recites his "promises," followed by the bride, and no third party is needed to pronounce the couple married (since it's believed only God can sanction the union).

The Civil Ceremony

A civil ceremony is nonreligious and can be performed practically anywhere—in a private home or club, or in a judge's chambers or city clerk's office.

Who can perform one? A justice of the peace, a judge, governor, ship's captain, some notary publics, and some mayors and city clerks. Check first with the local marriage-license bureau or municipal clerk's office, since regulations differ among counties. In some counties, a judge can legally officiate at a civil ceremony, but not a justice of the peace.

A bride is free to wear a long formal gown at a civil ceremony, but many choose instead to wear a suit or simple dress and jacket ensemble if the ceremony will be held in an office setting.

Double Wedding Ceremony

Two siblings? Two sisters? A double wedding can be an economical way for two couples to share wedding expenses, especially if they will be inviting the same guests anyway. Most double weddings are held for two sisters, two brothers, or a brother and sister; but it's possible to hold one with sets of close friends.

Usually, the older bride goes down the aisle first. The brides may choose to share attendants or have entirely different bridal parties. This is not the kind of ceremony for a bride or groom who enjoys being the absolute center of attention, since the spotlight is shared.

Military Ceremony

A military wedding is appropriate only when either the bride or groom is an active or retired member of the armed forces. I found this out when I wanted to be married in the chapel at West Point Military Academy, where I had spent many childhood days. My father is a retired army colonel, and even though the reception was held at the West Point Officer's Club, where he has been a member for years, I couldn't have the ceremony in a post chapel, because technically neither my fiancé nor I was the military person in the family.

Check with the protocol officer on post or base before planning a military wedding. Usually the groom and any military attendants wear their dress uniforms during the ceremony. The bride may wear a wedding gown or her dress uniform. Following the ceremony, the couple walk through an honor-guard arch created by military attendants who hoist swords, sabers, or rifles.

193

Candlelight and Unity Candle Ceremonies

In a candlelight ceremony, the entire house of worship is illuminated by flickering candles. This creates a dreamy, romantic effect. Be sure to check with your officiant before planning one: There may be special fire ordinances and restrictions on where candles may be used. (Be wary of drafts and air conditioning that can cause accidents.) Also, the photographer will need to adjust for low-light conditions.

The unity candle ceremony symbolizes the newly joined couple. After the couple exchange vows, they each take a candle and light it from the flame of one larger candle on the altar.

Sometimes each guest is also given a candle at the beginning of the ceremony. The couple walk down the aisle, stopping at each row to light the candle of the nearest person, who in turn lights the candle of the next person, until the entire congregation has lighted candles—and the community is joined.

"We were married on October 15. After the reception, we went to a dance club, still dressed in our formal wedding clothes. Everyone was looking at us. One gentleman thought we were dressed early for Halloween. It was amusing! Our wedding was special. My mother had passed away four months earlier, which was hard. But when my father gave me away and the minister asked, 'Who gives this bride?' my dad said, 'Her mother and I!' It brought tears to my eyes."

—Jodie LaMarre, Florida October bride

The Vessel and the Rose Ceremony

This ceremony, written by Rev. Roger Coleman, a Protestant minister and president of Clergy Services, Inc., in Kansas City, Missouri, highlights marriage as a lifelong relationship that is always in the making.

In it, a clay vessel symbolizes love's strength and endurance, and the power of God as the creator (in Genesis, the "Lord formed the human from the clay of the ground"). The rose symbolizes the potential and beauty contained in love's promises.

The officiant hands the vessel to the groom, and the bride places the rose in the vessel, which the bride and groom hold together and proclaim their desire to love and grow together.

The Family Medallion Ceremony

Also developed by Rev. Roger Coleman, this ceremony is intended for including children in a ceremony when parents marry following divorce or the death of a spouse. In it, after the newlyweds exchange rings, their children join them at the altar. A family ceremony follows, in which the bride and groom place a sterling-silver medal around the neck of each child. Then they pledge their love to their children.

A WEDDING DAY BLESSING

May the blessing of light be with you always

Light without and light within

May the sun shine upon you and warm your heart

Until it glows like a great fire

So that others may feel the warmth of it

And may the light of your eyes

Shine like two candle lights

In a window at night bidding the wanderer

To come in out of the dark and the cold

And may the blessings of the rain be upon you

The sweet and tender rain

May it fall upon your spirit

As when flowers spring up and fragrance fills the air

And may the blessings of the great rain

Wash you clean and fair,

And may the storms always leave you stronger

And more beautiful

And when the rains are over

May there be clear pools of water

Made beautiful by the radiance of your light

As when a star shines beautiful in the night

Pointing the way for all of us

(Reprinted with permission of Rev. Roger Coleman.)

WRITING YOUR OWN VOWS

How will you say "I do?"

Many couples today who want their ceremony to be really meaningful and personal are writing their own vows.

"When people get married, they search for just the right words to express feelings and intentions of the heart," notes Rev. Randy Mayeux, pastor of the interdenominational Christ Church North in Dallas. "Every couple I see wants a mixture of the traditional readings woven together with the contemporary."

These days, officiants and bridal consultants are often called upon to help couples write their own vows or find special ways to include loved ones and children from a previous marriage in the ceremony.

Before trying to write a new ceremony from start to finish, keep in mind that many houses of worship impose restrictions on where—and if—you can tinker with the script. This is an important consideration. There are sometimes

197

complex rules about who walks in with whom, or special prayers or procedures that are inviolate if the ceremony is to be legally and/or religiously binding.

For details about the specific content for your denomination, always meet with the officiant first. He or she may have lists of readings to choose from or suggestions for ways to personalize it all.

Sometimes, special wordings, sentiments, or poems may be recited before or after the vows are exchanged. This reflects your commitment to each other or personal references to where you met or fell in love.

Following the ring exchange, the bride might add: "Jim, I promise to celebrate your many strengths, be tolerant of your weaknesses, and love you for all my life with enduring affection, support and humor."

Or the groom might say: "Sally, ever since I met you in the college library, I knew in my heart you were the only woman for me. Come grow old with me and be my loving partner."

Not surprisingly, modern couples have overwhelmingly dropped the traditional "love, honor, and obey" portion of the ceremony for the more politically correct "love, honor, and cherish."

Here's a Tip:
Couples who write their own vows often panic they'll forget them during the ceremony. Rev. Randy Mayeux suggests they type the words out and bring them along. The bride can stash her copy in her glove, and the groom can keep his in a pocket. It doesn't diminish the effect one bit if they read them.

Special Touches for the Ceremony:

❀ Doves, butterflies, or helium balloons released during the ceremony.

❀ Instead of throwing rice at the couple, guests throw birdseed, rose petals, popcorn, or even blow bubbles.

❀ Instead of a quick recessional, the bride and groom stop at each row and greet guests.

❀ Children or honored guests are invited to stand around the altar during the wedding vows.

❀ The bride and groom face the guests.

❀ The bride hands a rose to both mothers, or each guest.

❀ The bride walks down an aisle runner made entirely of fresh rose petals! Wedding consultant Annena Sorenson suggests arranging for a wholesale florist to order an entire case of petals for a thick, solid "blanket." The effect is truly spectacular.

Questions to Ask the Officiant

❀ Are there any restrictions on wedding attire (no bare shoulders or back, veil mandatory, and so on)?

❀ May we write or choose sections of the ceremony, such as our vows or favorite religious passages?

❀ Must all readings be religious?

❀ Can we include family or ethnic traditions?

199

❀ Are there prohibitions on photography during the ceremony? If not, where may the photographer/videographer stand? Is the use of special lighting or flashbulbs prohibited?

❀ Can we bring in our own soloist or organist, or must we use the house performer?

❀ Are guests allowed to throw rice? birdseed? flower petals? Inside the sanctuary or out on steps?

❀ Can you suggest ways to include children or special guests in the ceremony?

❀ What is the procedure for signing the marriage license and marriage certificate? How many witnesses are needed?

❀ Do we do this before or after the ceremony?

❀ What is the fee for performing the ceremony?

❀ Where can we hold the receiving line?

❀ Will the entire wedding ceremony be printed in a bulletin or program (to make it easy for guests to follow)?

❀ For a Catholic officiant: Does this church allow non-Catholics to take Communion?

❀ Are there restrictions on music for the ceremony?

❀ May we hold a candlelight ceremony?

❀ Are any accessories provided (aisle runner, pew decorations, chuppah, candelabra)?

❀ Is there a special place for the bride and bridesmaids to prepare for the ceremony?

❀ We are planning an interfaith ceremony. How can we arrange for officiants from both our faiths to co-officiate?

❀ Can you explain the order of the processional and recessional to us?

❀ When can we schedule a dress rehearsal for the ceremony?

CUSTOM AND CEREMONY

Something old, something new, something borrowed, and something blue . . . and a copper penny in your shoe! Most brides-to-be know this classic wedding rhyme by heart, the time-honored "formula" for marital fidelity, prosperity, and bliss.

Like most rituals, the wedding ceremony is steeped in symbolism and superstition. Even couples who don't place much stock in tradition often find themselves taking the old wives' tales and folklore awfully seriously when it comes to wedding planning. Following these customs is a way of fostering family unity by repeating steps taken by family and friends before you. And for those who believe one can never be "too sure," it's a protection of sorts against bad luck. After all, why tempt fate?

Many of the wedding customs we recognize today have evolved from religious symbolism. The smashing of the cloth-wrapped wineglass in a Jewish ceremony signals the end of the wedding ceremony, serves as a reminder of the destruction of the Holy Temple in Israel, and reminds us that love is fragile and must be protected.

Other customs are more secular in origin. Did you know that shopping for

201

a wedding trousseau recalls the ancient French custom of the bride carrying a bundle *(trousse)* of her clothing and possessions to her new home?

Many wedding traditions date back to the time when people believed in the existence of evil spirits—powerful entities who could bring death and disease and wreak havoc on crops. Since agriculture was the basis of most primitive economies, one didn't want to mess with the demons! Newlyweds—and brides in particular—were believed to be singled out by evil spirits for harm or mischief, and the bride and groom together were deemed to be especially ripe targets. Hence, it was considered unlucky for the groom to even see the bride on their wedding day. (Imagine, it meant the spirits had access to them both in one place!) As a safeguard, in some cultures a curtain was even placed between the bride and groom during the ceremony.

Why Does the Bride Choose Bridesmaids?

The practice of inviting friends to "attend" the couple, and dress just like them, was intended to confuse the evil spirits. Furthermore, in ancient Roman times, it was legally required that at least ten attendants be witnesses to make a wedding contract legal.

Why Does the Bride Wear a Wedding Veil?

Blame it on those spirits again. By concealing her face, it was believed the evil spirits couldn't tell which maiden was the bride. Early Greek and Roman brides wore red or yellow veils, because these colors were thought to represent fire and act as a powerful protection against demons. Today in some cultures, the white veil is a symbol of modesty and virginity.

Why Does the Groom Choose Ushers?

Like bridesmaids, the groomsmen were invited to confuse the spirits and prevent them from harming the couple. Some say this tradition may also date back to the days of "marriage by capture," when the groom literally carried off a bride, and his warrior buddies helped defend him against anybody who objected (including the bride and her parents)!

Why Does the Couple Have a Honeymoon?

The groom who "captured" his bride often kept her hidden for a full month (or "moon"), during which time they partied and drank a honey-sweetened alcoholic drink believed to loosen up sexual inhibitions. Even couples who married amicably were encouraged to take some time to themselves, to adjust to their newly married status and forget the worries of the world, at least for a short time.

203

Why Does the Groom Stand on the Bride's Right Side at the Altar?

It supposedly leaves his right hand—the sword hand—free to protect her from rejected suitors or anyone who might kidnap her or do her harm.

Why Is a Wedding "Sealed" with a Kiss?

The wedding kiss was believed to represent an exchange of spirits in which a part of one's soul joined the spouse's soul and the newlyweds were truly united as one. In some cultures, the kiss was literally considered a legal bond that sealed the marriage contract.

Why Wear a Wedding Ring? And Why on a Certain Finger?

Eternal love! Because of its circular shape, a ring has always been a symbol of unending love. The early Egyptians wore wedding rings made of woven rushes or hemp. Since these natural fibers wore out with use, the ring had to be constantly replaced. ("Honey, it's time for *another* wedding ring!") The ancient Greeks and Romans used more sturdy rings of iron or gold, which also displayed the wealth of the bridegroom.

In ancient cultures, the ring was placed on the third finger of the left hand because it was believed that the vein in that finger led directly to the heart. Most brides today still observe this practice, but in some parts of Europe the traditional ring finger is on the right hand. And in some communities around the world, the bride wears her ring on the left hand while engaged and then moves it to the right hand when married.

Why Does the Bride Wear a White Gown?

In modern times a gown has come to symbolize a wide variety of things—joy, fertility, and celebration. In some cultures, a white gown is also associated with virginity.

But brides haven't always worn white. Over the centuries, brides have worn their best dress or national costume on their wedding day. In Colonial America, a bride often wore a homespun calico, her "Sunday best," or even a sober blue, black, or brown dress.

In the 1840s, when England's Queen Victoria got married in a white wedding gown (instead of the traditional royal silver), white dresses suddenly became the rage. The white gown also became a symbol of wealth, since most women couldn't afford a dress they would wear only a few times. Without modern-day conveniences, cleaning a pure white dress that elaborate was next to impossible.

Why Does the Bride Carry a Bouquet? And Why Toss It in the Air?

Some historians credit this custom with the ancient Roman practice of carrying bunches of fragrant herbs and flowers on the wedding day to ward off evil spirits. (Imagine having a garlic bouquet!)

The Greeks carried ivy as a symbol of unending love. Modern custom has evolved so that tossing the bouquet is now a predictor of the next woman to be married and a symbol of the bride embracing her new life. But in ancient times, it was believed a bride was especially lucky on her wedding day, so guests would often tear at the bride's clothing to get a keepsake piece. Tossing the bouquet and garter were believed to prevent this mob scene and keep the crowd happy—and at bay.

Other wedding historians say the garter toss is a throwback to the old British custom of "flinging the stocking." On the wedding night, guests would follow the happy couple back to their bedroom, wait until they had undressed, steal their stockings—then fling them at the couple. The first person to hit the bride or groom on the head was the next person to wed. (Some say the precise target was the bride or groom's nose, other versions have the guests hurling their own stockings at the couple, but you get the picture.)

205

And Why Something Old, Something New, Something Borrowed and Something Blue?

These practices are all meant to ensure a happy and lasting marriage. Carrying something old and something new symbolizes a sense of continuity while making a transition to a new life. The color blue has long been associated with purity and modesty. In ancient Israel, blue was the border color of a bride's dress and denoted constancy and fidelity. By borrowing something from a happily married woman, it was believed her good fortune would rub off on the bride. And the penny in the shoe? It symbolizes good fortune and protection against want.

MODERN CUSTOMS FROM AROUND THE WORLD

Today, many American couples are choosing to incorporate wedding ceremony and reception traditions derived from their own ethnic roots or in homage to the heritage of their grandparents or great-grandparents. It's a wonderful way to preserve the past while making the passage to a new, shared life together.

African-American Traditions

During the days of slavery, when slaves were forbidden to marry, a man and woman declared their marriage vows by jumping over a broom. The broom symbolized a sort of threshold and the beginning of a new life. Many contemporary couples are choosing to "jump the broom" too.

Another revived tradition is for the bride to wear intricately braided hair, often decorated with cowrie shells or pieces of silver, and for the couple to wear traditional African robes in kente or asooke cloth made of colorful geometric patterns.

Some African-American weddings today also feature the traditional rite of winding plaited grass around the couple's wrists, to symbolize their union.

Hispanic Traditions

During the ceremony, thirteen gold coins (representing the groom's dowry to the bride and his promise to support her) are carried in a box or tray and blessed by the priest, then passed back and forth between the hands of the bride and groom until they rest with the bride.

A large rosary or white rope called a *laso* is wound around the couple's shoulders in a figure eight during the wedding ceremony, to symbolize their union. Sometimes an heirloom mantilla is used in place of the *laso*.

Three wedding bouquets are used: one is carried by the bride, one is left at the altar in honor of the Virgin Mary, and the third is tossed at the ceremony.

The "dollar dance" is a traditional custom in which money is pinned to the bride's dress by each man who dances with her.

Jewish Traditions

In the Jewish wedding ceremony, the smashing of a cloth-wrapped wineglass signals the end of the marriage ceremony, as a reminder of the hardship endured by the Jewish people by the destruction of the Holy Temple in ancient Israel, and as a reminder of the fragility of love and marriage. Wedding consultant Denise Winkelstein suggests using a pretty fabric "mazel tov" bag trimmed to match the bride's gown that is filled with a light bulb rather than a glass—much easier to break.

207

Japanese Traditions

The bride and her parents visit the groom's house on the wedding day. She wears a traditional ceremonial kimono as a wedding gown and may change out of it for the wedding banquet.

Nine sips of sake are drunk by the bride and groom during the ceremony. They are considered married after the first sip!

Italian Traditions

The couple walks through the village on their wedding day, doling out cakes and sweets to guests, or they give sweets (called "confetti") as party favors to guests at the reception. Confetti isn't tiny bits of paper, but rather sugared almonds. Sometimes referred to as Jordan almonds, these represent both fertility and the bitter and sweet aspects of life. The almonds are traditionally wrapped in tulle fabric and tied with a colorful bow. Sometimes the tulle packet includes three almonds, symbolizing two parents and a child.

A white silk or satin purse called a *busta,* usually decorated with lace, is carried by the bride at the wedding reception to store wedding cards and envelopes bearing gifts of money. While in some cultures wedding gifts of money are considered inappropriate or even tacky, in the Italian tradition money gifts are considered a thoughtful way to help the couple get established financially.

Often, a traditional Italian folk dance called the tarantella is performed by the guests at the reception.

Irish Traditions

The groom is lifted high up in a chair (called a "jaunting car") at the reception, to signify he is now a married man.

For good luck, the couple is given a horseshoe to display in their new home.

New Year's Day is considered the luckiest day of the year to be married.

The traditional Irish wedding ring is the Claddagh ring, which is decorated with two hands holding a heart and a crown above them. The heart, crown, and hands symbolize love, loyalty, and friendship, respectively.

The traditional Irish wedding cake is a fruitcake.

German Traditions

Both bride and groom wear engagement rings in the form of gold bands.

During the wedding ceremony, the groom kneels on the hem of the bride's gown to symbolize his control over her. In return, as the bride rises, she asserts her power over him by stepping on his foot.

On the night before the wedding, a *polterabend* tradition is for the guests to break crockery and play tricks on the couple. *Abend* means "night" in German, and the word *polterabend* is derived from "poltergeist," or noisy, playful ghost or spirit.

Greek Traditions

During the wedding ceremony, the bride and groom wear crowns of flowers, which are placed on their heads by an honored male guest known as the *koumbaros*. The couple walk around the altar three times, symbolizing the Holy Trinity.

Scottish Traditions

The groom gives the bride an engraved silver teaspoon on their wedding day, as a promise they will never go hungry. Sometimes a traditional sword dance is performed at the reception.

English Traditions

Bridesmaids are usually young girls, not women. (Remember the wedding of Prince Charles and Lady Diana Spencer? All the bridesmaids were little girls.)

The traditional wedding cake is a dense, rich fruitcake, usually soaked in spirits and wrapped in a sweet fondant icing.

The bride often sews a good-luck charm into the hem of her dress. Princess Diana's dress had a tiny horseshoe hidden in the hem, the good-luck charm favored by royalty.

Polish Traditions

Guests who dance with the bride at the reception are expected to place gifts of money in the pocket of an apron she wears for the occasion, or pin money to her dress.

When the bride is dressed and ready to put on her veil, she stands by a mirror and watches her mother put it on for her. This symbolizes the last task a mother does for her little girl, before she becomes a woman with her own life.

Chinese Traditions

The wedding color scheme always includes a warm color to signify happiness. Red is considered the color of love and joy, so the bride may wear a red wedding dress.

Customs and traditions are always evolving—which means it's perfectly okay to establish your own family traditions. A wedding is the perfect time to begin a new family legacy.

⊛ Have a wedding program printed up listing the wedding date, time, liturgy, honored guests, and any special message you hope to share with guests. When Tref Lowe was married to John Barillo in Indianapolis, their wedding program honored the memory of recently deceased family members and friends and also included inspirational messages about love by author Leo Buscaglia. They also included a thank-you message to all those who had traveled a long distance to take part in their wedding.

❀ Incorporate heirloom family lace into the wedding veil or gown. Some brides are even saving the lace from their gown to fashion into a christening outfit for future generations.

❀ Incorporate part of the bride's mother's wedding dress into a going-away outfit for the bride, suggests photographer Gregory Geiger of Orange, Connecticut, especially if the dress hasn't been preserved well enough for the bride to wear as her own wedding gown.

❀ Have your parents' wedding albums on display at the reception, Geiger also suggests, and use their original cake knife to cut the cake. Have the bride and groom's names and wedding dates engraved on the handle, along with the parents' dates. This makes a wonderful memento to pass along to children and grandchildren.

❀ Take a photograph of all the children invited to the wedding. Make copies and present one to each child in years hence, when he or she marries.

❀ Save the candles from the wedding ceremony and relight them during special family occasions such as the first anniversary, the birth of a child, or the marriage of a brother or sister.

❀ At the ceremony, ask each guest to sign fabric squares or a large tablecloth with indelible-ink pens. The squares can be sewn into a keepsake quilt or the tablecloth used on each anniversary.

Music for the Ceremony and Reception

What does wedding music mean to you?
Is it a traditional organ rendition of "Here Comes the Bride"?
A love song crooned by a folk singer with guitar?
Or an energetic band that doesn't stop till the last guest drops?

Because a wedding is both ceremony and celebration, it's important to give careful consideration to the kind of music you favor. The right music adds ambience and creates an atmosphere that enhances the ceremony or puts guests in a festive mood for celebrating.

Many couples put off music decisions until the end of wedding planning because they find it overwhelming and don't know what to ask or where to begin. By the time they get around to choosing a band, they may have exhausted the wedding budget, or else the musicians may already be booked elsewhere.

It's a good idea to book a band or group as early as possible—at least six to twelve months ahead.

Music fees vary widely across the country and are generally higher in big cities. For about four hours of live entertainment, expect to spend anywhere from $400 to $600 for a small, relatively unknown group to upward of $5,000 to $10,000 for a multipiece, established orchestra.

According to professional wedding planners, bands tend to charge top dollar for Saturday nights, New Year's Eve, or anytime during the month of December, when business and private holiday parties create more demand for entertainers.

Before hiring a band, listen to it first, either live or on a demonstration tape. Music and talent agencies often provide demo tapes in the form of cassettes or videotapes. These feature a variety of entertainers and band styles for a nice sampler.

Some band leaders will invite couples to hear them play at another wedding or private party, while others feel this is an invasion of privacy. (Would *you* like it if some stranger hung around your wedding?) When checking out groups at someone else's affair, be sure to dress appropriately and keep a very low profile.

"I would say it's a waste of time to listen to a band play at someone else's party because the band is simply playing what *that* client wanted," music consultant Jessica Siegel, owner of An Angel's Touch Music Service in Walnut Creek, California, notes. A good way to hear a band perform live without crashing someone else's party is to attend an "audition night," a private show for prospective clients.

Remember, a demonstration tape may provide the flavor of a band's style, but these tapes are professionally produced, and unless you specify it in the contract there is no guarantee that the band you hear is the one you'll get for your wedding. Be sure to ask about this.

A demo tape, moreover, can't showcase all the music styles a band can play. Ask how versatile they are and whether they can do all the styles you want— such as Big Band, golden oldies, pop tunes, ethnic music, Latin beat, rhythm and blues, jazz, classical music, and so on.

Some groups will provide a suggested "playlist" of music popular for weddings. You can always add your personal favorites, too. Be sure to include music in a variety of styles to appeal to an audience of different age groups.

WHERE TO BEGIN

Overwhelmed by all the music styles and selections out there? A good place to start is by viewing the *Here Comes the Bride* music video from MBC Video (see appendix). In it is footage from more than forty-five real weddings with real couples in a variety of religious and civil ceremonies. Featured are examples of different instrumentation ensembles so you get an idea, for example, of what a string quartet, harpist, or harpsichord-and-flute duo sound like. And while each piece of music is playing, the work's composer, title, and number are flashed across the screen. The tape is accompanied by a list of the songs, by number, for easy reference later.

Another good place to start is to think about the location of the ceremony and reception and how many guests will attend. What is the theme of the wedding? How big is your budget? Are there special family considerations or ethnic traditions to uphold? In the Rienzo family, a party isn't considered a party unless Great-Uncle George, an eighty-year-old practicing psychiatrist, sings "Life Is Just a Bowl of Cherries." The tradition is so long-standing, nobody remembers how or why it even began.

Location is an important consideration; many churches, synagogues, and reception sites place restrictions on the choice of music (sacred versus secular) and may prohibit amplified music or a band larger than a few pieces.

Will the wedding be held in a private home or residential neighborhood? The neighbors may not appreciate musicians playing till midnight or two in the morning.

Geography can also set limitations. It's impractical to lug a cumbersome instrument like a harp or piano up endless flights of stairs in a historic mansion or deep into the woods at a public park. These logistical considerations seem obvious but are easy to overlook.

The number of guests invited is another factor. Hiring a fifteen-piece band to entertain twenty-five guests is overkill. A general rule of thumb in the industry is to hire a three-piece band for small weddings; a five-piece band for weddings of a hundred guests or more; and a seven-piece band or large orchestra for groups of more than a hundred. Add another piece for each increment of fifty guests.

Short on time? Consider hiring a band through an agency. There are advantages. An agency has already prescreened a wide variety of musical groups and knows which ones are dependable, have played at weddings, and work well under pressure.

You can also locate musical groups through other sources such as the yellow pages, local musicians' union, referrals from other couples, and wedding vendors such as the caterer and/or reception site manager. Scan the society pages in the local newspaper for groups that have played at charity balls or fund-raising events. Or call the local music school or conservatory for referrals to student performers.

The Orchestra Leaders Association (see appendix), will provide a list of member bands in your area and advice on choosing the right size and style band for your function. The association upholds standards of professionalism, talent, and quality.

Limited budget? Consider booking a disc jockey or one-man-band musician who electronically replicates the sound of many instruments with a synthesizer computer. A disc jockey usually arrives with a sound system and a wide assortment of music on tape, albums, or compact disc. Some disc jockeys will also act as master of ceremonies for the reception and/or provide light shows, costumed dancers, or bubble machines that release floaty bubbles as the music plays. But don't assume a disc jockey is always cheaper than a live musical group.

Another inexpensive alternative is to hire the musicians to do double duty at the ceremony and reception. It's cheaper than booking separate groups. Or call the local music school for student referrals. Another low-cost option is to create your own long-playing tape of favorites.

217

MUSIC FOR THE CEREMONY

When choosing music for the wedding ceremony, keep in mind that a ceremony usually has several parts, each of which calls for a different tone.

The Prelude

The prelude is the thirty- to forty-five-minute period before the bride arrives, when guests are filing in and taking their seats. Many couples feel that soothing, unobtrusive selections set the tone for this reflective time, and so favor chamber music selections, lilting folk music, romantic contemporary tunes, or Chopin preludes.

Remember, too, if the ceremony is in a house of worship, there may be restrictions on the kind of music you choose. The officiant may already have lists of appropriate musical selections on hand, with referrals to local musicians. If you're going to spring for a vocalist or ensemble, schedule it for later in the ceremony, when everyone has arrived and will actually *hear* it. Sometimes, if you choose to hire your own performers instead of using the "house" organist or vocalist, you may actually be charged an entertainment fee for them anyway. Check it out.

The Processional

The processional begins when the mother of the bride is seated and the bride commences her walk down the aisle. This calls for uplifting music that places the bride at center stage! There is no law that says the bride must walk down the aisle to strains from *Lohengrin* but do choose something that evokes a sense of fanfare.

The Ceremony Itself

Music can maintain a joyous mood throughout the ceremony, emphasize the religious meaning of the ceremony, or encourage guest participation. A combination of vocal and instrumental music is a nice touch, whether that means hiring a choir, a soloist (vocalist, violinist, flautist, harpist, organist), or asking a talented friend or relative to perform. Again, it's wise to check with the officiant about music restrictions during a mass or religious ceremony. When selecting hymns, be sure to provide the lyrics for guests to read and follow. Avoid overly long hymns or verses that might be inappropriate for a wedding. And yes, it's perfectly okay to play "your song" or a contemporary pop tune during the ceremony (as long as it won't pop the guests' eardrums). After all, a wedding is a personalized celebration.

The Recessional

At long last, the big moment! The bride and groom kiss, are pronounced husband and wife, and begin their walk back up the aisle as a married couple. The recessional calls for lively and celebratory music—nothing too slow or somber—because couples invariably get caught up in their joy and sprint up the aisle together. It's a nice touch for the music to continue until all the guests have filed out and joined the receiving line.

219

Possible Selections

Classical

"Bridal Chorus" (from *Lohengrin*, by Wagner; also known as
"Here Comes the Bride")

"Church Sonata" in C (Mozart)

"Trumpet Voluntary" (Purcell)

"The Wedding March," recessional (from a *Midsummer Night's Dream*,
by Mendelssohn)

"Canon in D Minor" (Pachelbel)

"Ave Maria" (Schubert)

"Jesu, Joy of Man's Desiring" (J. S. Bach)

"Now Thank We All Our God" (Johnson)

"Ode to Joy" (Beethoven)

"Wedding March" (Guilmant)

"Water Music" suite (Handel)

"A Wedding Processional" (Near)

Contemporary (recommended recordings)

"You Are So Beautiful" (Joe Cocker)

"Evergreen" (Barbra Streisand)

"The Wedding Song (And There Is Love)" (Paul Stookey)

"Follow Me" (John Denver)

"Wind Beneath My Wings" (Bette Midler)

"I Will Always Love You" (Dolly Parton)

"First Time Ever I Saw Your Face" (Roberta Flack)

"Let It Be" (John Lennon and Paul McCartney)

"Morning Has Broken" (Cat Stevens)

"Time in a Bottle" (Jim Croce)

"You Light Up My Life" (Debby Boone)

"The Rose" (Bette Midler)

MUSIC FOR THE RECEPTION AND FIRST DANCE
(Recommended Recordings)

"We've Only Just Begun" (Paul Williams)

"Chances Are" (Johnny Mathis)

"Every Move You Make" (Sting)

"True Companion" (Marc Cohn)

"Because of You" (Tony Bennett)

"You Are the Sunshine of My Life" (Stevie Wonder)

"Till There Was You" (Paul McCartney)

"People" (Barbra Streisand)

"I Get a Kick Out of You" (Frank Sinatra)

"My Heart Belongs to Daddy" (Cole Porter)

"A Whole New World" (from Disney's *Aladdin*)

"Just the Way You Are" (Billy Joel)

"If I Loved You" (by Rogers and Hammerstein)

"You Needed Me" (Anne Murray)

"Can't Help Falling in Love" (Elvis Presley)

"I Don't Know Much" (Linda Ronstadt)

"Endless Love" (Diana Ross)

"The Hands of Time" (Michel LeGrand)

"Follow Me" (Peter, Paul and Mary)

"Unchained Melody" (Righteous Brothers)

"You're in My Heart, You're in My Soul" (Rod Stewart)

"If Tomorrow Never Comes" (Garth Brooks)

"I Swear" (John Michael Montgomery)

"On Bended Knee" (Boyz II Men)

"Pretty Woman" (Roy Orbison)

"Shut Up and Kiss Me" (Mary Chapin Carpenter)

"Night and Day" (by Cole Porter)

221

"Vision of Love" (Mariah Carey)

"Someone to Watch over Me" (by George Gershwin)

"We Must Be in Love" (Pure Soul)

Folk, Line, and Circle Dance Music

"Achy, Breaky Heart" (Billy Ray Cyrus)

"The Alley Cat"

The tarantella

The Irish jig

The horah

Texas two-step

The tush push

Boot stompin' boogie

"Turkey in the Straw" (square dance)

"At the Copacabana" (conga music, Barry Manilow)

Electric slide

Indiana earthquake

Who'll Play It?

Traditional band or orchestra

Rock band

Taped music

Harpist

Disc jockey

Chamber ensemble

Pianist

Square-dance music

Country-western band

A cappella group

One-man band

Mariachi band

Rap group

Madrigal singers

Caribbean steel band

Organist

Violinist

High school or college choral group

Barbershop quartet

Strolling violinists

Woodwind trio or quartet

Karaoke

Bagpiper(s)

Guitarist

FACE THE MUSIC: QUESTIONS TO ASK THE BAND

- ❂ Do they have a demo tape?

- ❂ Do they carry liability insurance (in case, say, a guest trips over a wire or bandstand)?

- ❂ Where can you hear the band perform live?

- ❂ Will the band you've auditioned be the same band that will play at your wedding?

- ❂ How will the band members be attired?

- ❂ What is the fee? Is it lower on certain days of the week or seasons of the year?

- ❂ When is the deposit due? How much? When is the balance due?

- ❂ What are the overtime charges?

- ❂ When do overtime charges begin?

- ❂ Does the band take requests from guests?

- ❂ How many members will play at the wedding? What instruments?

- ❂ How long have these particular musicians played together?

- ❂ Where else have they appeared?

- ❀ How long has the band been performing at weddings?

- ❀ Does the band work from a predetermined playlist or do they determine the "feel" of the audience and tailor their playlist on site?

- ❀ Does the band encourage audience participation?

- ❀ Has the band scheduled another wedding for the same day?

- ❀ Do the musicians have special equipment or electrical needs (extra outlets, extension cords, music stands, podium)?

- ❀ Does the bandleader act as a master of ceremonies and announce the special events throughout the reception (cake cutting, garter throw, bouquet toss)?

- ❀ What kind of food and beverages do they expect?

- ❀ When, and how often, do they schedule breaks?

- ❀ What is the band's musical specialty?

- ❀ Will they provide continuous taped music during their breaks?

For nearly twenty years, Mikki Viereck performed at weddings and felt something important was missing. "Daddy's Little Girl" was a familiar staple of most receptions, and the father of the bride got to dance a sentimental dance with his daughter, but there was no comparable tune for the mother of the groom, says the singer and songwriter from Massachusetts.

So Viereck wrote one. The result was "Song for My Son," a ballad in waltz time. ("I don't know where/The time has gone/Since those little boy days/Doesn't seem that long/Yet here you are/It's your wedding day.")

"Moms would always ask why there is no song for mothers and sons," recalls Viereck, herself the mother of two sons. "I could understand. They wanted special words for their son on the day he gets married."

The first time she sang "Song for My Son" at a wedding, all the mothers in the room ended up with handkerchiefs to their eyes.

"A Song for My Son" has since been released on compact disc and cassette and sold nationwide. It has been performed on NBC's *Today* show and ABC's *Home Show.*

But Viereck didn't stop there. Requests kept pouring in for contemporary wedding songs devoted to mothers and daughters—and so she penned the lyrics to "A Song for My Daughter."

Her public wanted even more. Couples asked her for a wedding song they could use to thank their loved ones, and "A Wedding Thank You" was written. When the requests turned to a more dignified alternative to the traditional "Farmer in the Dell" cake-cutting tune, she wrote another new song called "As We Break This Bread Together."

"As We Break This Bread" has a beautiful classic sound, and some people are using it in the Christian ceremony for the communion song, and others of the Jewish faith for the blessing of the bread, Viereck notes.

Viereck's company, New Traditions Publishing ASCAP, has now released New Wedding Traditions, an album of new wedding music with words and music written by Viereck, Steve Moser, and Bob Casinghino. "Weddings are about sentiment, love, and tradition," Viereck says. "What better way to relay a message of love than through a song?"

225

Chapter Fourteen

The Reception and Catering

Where will you hold the celebration of a lifetime?

For most couples, this is the ultimate planning question, because the wedding date itself hinges on securing a reception site and caterer. Once the reception is booked, everything seems to fall into place.

Not surprisingly, many couples arrange for a reception site and then work backward, securing a ceremony location for that day. That's because reception sites are often reserved more than a year in advance, and special events—like political conventions or the World Cup soccer tournament—can monopolize hotel space and party planners.

When the World Cup soccer tournament scheduled games in Chicago, even brides who had never heard of soccer before were affected. Hotels were fully booked up—which meant brides couldn't reserve reception sites and guests couldn't get hotel accommodations—and many weddings were shifted from June to September.

You and your fiancé should first discuss the size and formality of a reception that suits your taste and budget. Think carefully about the tone and atmosphere you want to create. Will it be a themed wedding, an ultraformal extravaganza, or a casual garden party for close friends? The important thing is that the celebration reflects your personal tastes, not the vision of a parent or professional consultant who says you "must" do this or that.

To find an unusual site, contact the local visitors' bureau or convention center. In New England, weddings held in historic mansions or on yachts are popular. Florida brides are fortunate to have miles of tropical beachfront as potential wedding territory. In California, the wine country offers spectacular scenery and wineries that open their doors for receptions.

The bonus of choosing a historic site is that most landmark properties feature unforgettable backdrops for photographs: a dramatic staircase, handpainted wall panels, landscaped courtyard, grand ballroom, or stained-glass windows.

Couples needn't spend a fortune to secure a memorable site. Consider having the wedding in a private home, public park with beautiful grounds, church or club hall, art gallery, tented field, or in a space at a college or university (alumni sometimes get reduced rates, too). You may need a city permit for park or beach parties. Many aquariums, zoos, and museums, too, are now opening up their facilities to private parties as a way to boost revenues during off-hours. (How about cocktails by the shark tank?) But be forewarned: When planning a reception in a tented site on the grounds of a home or club, keep all the little extras in mind that can add precipitously to the cost. "Creating" a site from scratch means all the amenities need to be brought in—including portable rest rooms, heating, air conditioning, cooking and refrigeration facilities, tables and chairs, decorations, and much more. (See sidebar.)

If cost is a factor, consider having a wedding during the week instead of on the weekend, or an off-season wedding (January through March) instead of a peak-season one (May through September). Yes, Virginia, it's okay to have a midweek wedding! Reception sites charge a premium for weekends, and even a Friday-night booking may cost less than one on a Saturday or Sunday.

For the best price, don't even think of planning a June wedding, because *everybody* wants to be a June bride. According to the Association of Bridal Consultants, about 12.6 percent of all weddings in America are held in June. June's prominence has stemmed from a variety of practical factors, including the historical fact that it was after the planting season but before the harvest— so people had time for such celebrations. And by June in early America, most dirt roads had dried up enough after the spring thaw to make travel possible.

September is the next-most-popular month (11.8 percent), followed by August (11.2 percent), May (10.1 percent, July (9.5 percent), and October (9.2 percent). January is the ugly duckling—only about 1 in 25 brides weds during the first month of the year.

LEVELS OF FORMALITY

Across the country, the terms *formal, very formal,* and *informal* mean different things. These descriptions are general and technically refer to type of wedding dress the bride wears (not necessarily the size or expense of the wedding).

Very Formal (sometimes called UltraFormal)

This is the most traditional—and usually most expensive—wedding, with every trimming imaginable. Invitations are engraved, on white or ivory paper (and include two envelopes and enclosure cards); the guest list runs to two hundred or more; the bride wears a full-length gown with long or short gloves, and cathedral (or shorter) train and veil; and the groom wears a cutaway tux or long jacket for day or tailcoat for evening. The ceremony is held in a church or synagogue, temple or club.

A very formal wedding boasts a bevy of attendants (up to a dozen!) including flower girls, ring bearers, ushers, and bridesmaids; and the bridesmaids wear long dresses and long gloves. Generally, there is one usher for every fifty guests. Expect a multicourse sit-down dinner and champagne toast, head table for the bridal party, live multipiece orchestra, and lavish floral displays for both the ceremony and reception site. In the northeast part of the United States, an ultraformal or formal wedding is usually scheduled around 4 or 4:30 in the afternoon. Formal weddings in the South, Midwest, and West often take place in the evening.

Formal

The bride wears a long gown (with any sleeve length) plus a veil or train, and the guest list is around seventy-five to two hundred guests. The groom may wear a tuxedo for night or a cutaway for day. There are fewer attendants (up to six). This wedding style also features all the trimmings, but on a less grand scale, including music, flowers, a ceremony held in a house of worship or club, and a served meal. Invitations are engraved, on white or ivory paper.

Semiformal

Invitations are printed on any colored paper and may include photographs or graphics. There are usually two or three attendants, and the bride may wear a knee-length dress for a daytime wedding or a long dress for an evening wedding. The ceremony may be held anywhere, and the reception may or may not include music and a full meal. Refreshments usually include beverages and a modest buffet. Decorations are usually simple. The guest list is generally under a hundred people.

Informal

The bride wears whatever she fancies, be it a street-length dress or a suit with coordinating hat. Handwritten invitations are appropriate, or guests may be invited with a casual phone call. Few informal weddings are held in the evening. The guest list is generally small (under fifty people), and the reception is simple, with perhaps wedding cake, punch, appetizers, and beverages served. No attendants are necessary, but there must be witnesses to make it all legal.

THEMED WEDDINGS

Once you've decided on a level of formality, you may wish to consider a wedding theme.

If exchanging vows in a traditional house of worship or hotel seems downright boring to you, consider a nontraditional wedding with an unusual theme or venue. Couples have been known to say "I Do!" on a sailboat, in a hot-air balloon, or during rush hour at Grand Central Terminal in New York City.

Wedding festivities that reflect the couple's interests and personalities make for unforgettable celebrations. Friends might not remember you served jumbo shrimp, but they'll never forget the wedding if everyone came in costume or the bridal party skied to the ceremony.

Consider having the ceremony on a beach, and then celebrate with a New England-style clambake; or in a barn, and party afterward with a square-dance reception. A seasoned party planner or wedding consultant can help handle the extra challenges of staging a reception at an offbeat site. Themed weddings are gaining in favor all across the nation. These are weddings in which the venue, menu, decorations, favors, linens, and entertainment have all been carefully chosen to create an image or convey a special mood.

Sometimes a site can have a dramatically different feel depending on how it has been decorated. When two Texas sisters were married two years apart, consultant Robbi Ernst III was on hand to coordinate both weddings—which were held in the same place. One sister chose a western theme; the other fancied a more upscale, sophisticated look. The site was a large dance hall in a corrugated-tin building.

"For one of them, we turned the hall into a barn with bales of hay, fence posts, and kerosene lanterns for the tables," Ernst recalls. "For the other, the same place was more elegant with crystal, candelabras, and silver. We brought in trellis work and lattices and put it all around the room with greenery, and we covered the walls with rolls and rolls of fabric."

As you will see, almost anything goes.

Halloween or Masked Ball Guests are invited to come in costume or wear decorated masks with feathers and sequins! Carve pumpkins for inexpensive, colorful centerpieces.

Snowball Wedding The bride wears white—and so does the groom, the guests, and everyone in the wedding party.

Black-and-White Wedding Picture the bride dressed in white, the groom in black, and the wedding party and guests dressed in black or white attire only. While once deemed taboo for wedding attire, black is now considered sophisticated and contemporary.

Nautical Wedding Everyone boards a sailboat, barge, or yacht for a wedding at sea. When marrying at sea, be sure to thoroughly investigate local laws with the officiant or city clerk's office. Some maritime ceremonies must be performed within a certain mile limit of the shore, or while in port.

Renaissance Wedding The bridal couple and guests dress in period medieval costumes, and the reception is hosted in a castle or large banquet hall. Entertainment is provided by a madrigal choir, jugglers, or lute player. The bride and groom make their getaway on—what else?—horseback.

Holiday Wedding What's your favorite holiday of the year? New Year's Eve? Valentine's Day? Christmas? Fourth of July? Pick one and plan a theme

233

around it. The bonus of a holiday wedding is that you can take advantage of festive decorations already in place, such as boughs of holly and evergreens or pumpkins and colorful leaves.

During the Christmas holidays, most churches and catering sites are already decorated with beautiful evergreen trees and candles. One Illinois couple chose a local inn known for its lavish holiday decorations. The staircase was wrapped in pine, with Christmas decorations and ribbons, and Christmas trees appeared every few feet along the hallways. There was even a sleigh pulled by a reindeer!

Valentine's Wedding Use "Love" stamps and arrange for the invitations to be postmarked in a town with a romantic name (like Kissimmee, Florida, or Romance, Arkansas). Invitations might be Victorian themed with old-fashioned lace trim. Ask the baker to create a heart-shaped wedding cake, and decorate lavishly with heart-shaped baskets, fragrant candles, and red and pink flowers and linens. For party favors, consider individual heart-shaped boxes of chocolate at each place setting.

Wedding Weekend Plan an entire weekend of festivities in a resort or special site including a Friday-night party, Saturday luncheon, and Saturday-evening ceremony and reception. On Sunday, join the guests for a brunch, followed by more group activities like a family reunion, winery tour, or sports tournament.

Progressive Wedding The couple lives in New York City, but the bride's family lives in Florida and the groom's relatives lives in Montana. What to do? In a progressive wedding, the couple are married in one city (often the bride's hometown) and celebrate with local guests there; then travel the next day or several weeks later to the groom's home, where they have a second civil ceremony or a reception hosted by the groom's parents. A small, third party may be held in the city where the couple lives.

Victorian Wedding Choose a romantic, historic site and decorate it with candles, swags of richly colored fabric, and flowers for a period look. The bride might carry a bouquet of flowers chosen for their symbolic meanings, or wear orange blossoms in her hair (as England's Queen Victoria did in the mid-1800s on her wedding day). Dance to traditional waltz music and wear a gown of vintage lace. Consider leaving the ceremony in a horse-drawn carriage for formal pictures in an old-fashioned English garden.

Destination Wedding Get away from it all and tie the knot in an exotic or romantic locale—without eloping or leaving loved ones behind. Also called a honeymoon or getaway wedding, the destination wedding is a popular trend in the '90s. After all, if everybody is traveling to one destination for the wedding, why not make it a truly special locale?

Some resort managers and wedding consultants specialize in destination weddings and will take care of every teensy detail —from travel arrangements, hotel accommodations, and invitations to finding a justice of the peace and ordering the flowers and cake. Popular destination wedding sites include Disneyland in California and Disneyworld in Florida; the Greek isles, Africa, Hawaii, and the Bahamas. (For more information, see chapter on honeymoons.)

"As part of Jewish wedding ritual, you do a service that honors the bridegroom on the Saturday before the wedding. We made a family decision that since we all wanted to do a run, we would have the service at the beach. We did a run where we printed up maps and had T-shirts that read THE WEDDING RUN, and the prize for crossing the finish line was breakfast, hosted by the bride's uncle and aunt. On Friday, we started the weekend officially with the groom planting a tree in honor of his bride. Then we had a rehearsal dinner at a country club hosted by the groom's family. On Saturday afternoon, the groom came to the house to check out the bride—to make sure the bride is the right one—because of what happened in the Biblical story of Jacob and Leah, where the groom married the wrong sister. Traditionally, you do it before the wedding, but we did it in our own way. The groom and groomsmen came and sang, and it was very joyous. We had so many out-of-town guests, and people really wanted to participate in the joy and rituals that have been important to us."

—Sandra Lefkowitz, mother of a Connecticut December bride

Possible Reception Sites

Marina or shipyard	Airplane hangar
Art gallery	Private club
Museum	Historic mansion
Aboard a sailboat or yacht	Botanical garden

College campus

Zoo

Cornfield

Nature preserve

Resort or spa

Corporate meeting facility

Beach

Pier overlooking the waves

Country inn

Amusement park

Train station

Disneyland or Disneyworld

School gymnasium or classroom

Winery

The spot where you met

Outdoor garden or
    indoor greenhouse

Public park

Aquarium or maritime center

Private home

Restaurant

Church hall

Skating rink

Racetrack

Amphitheater

Barn

Hotel

Ferryboat

Warehouse

Women's club

Department store (after hours)

Office building lobby or atrium

Theater or movie theater
    (often closed Mondays)

237

"The most spectacular wedding I ever attended was on a barge docked beneath the Brooklyn Bridge. Although the August day was humid and hazy, the comfortable air-conditioned barge gave the wedding and reception a glorious backdrop of lower Manhattan skyscrapers.

At this same reception, the bride and bridegroom showed their big-city sophistication by serving a selection of sushi—the presence of which nauseated some of the relatives and invited guests. The ironic thing was, the sushi was vegetarian, with a filling of cucumber and avocado, and didn't contain a trace of fish! I didn't need to see or smell the raw fish. The back-and-forth rocking of the barge alone was enough to make me seasick, and I was surprised that more guests weren't green in the face, as I was."

—Steve Freitag, wedding guest

Questions to Ask a Reception Site Manager

- ❀ Do you provide catering, or just site rental?

- ❀ Is the fee based on use of certain rooms or floors of the facility only?

- ❀ Is there enough space for a dance floor?

- ❀ Do we need to provide a portable dance floor?

- ❀ Has our caterer ever worked in this site before?

- ❀ Are there rooms available for the wedding party to change into going-away attire?

- ❀ Can the site be used for both the ceremony and the reception?

- ❀ Is there a special place for the receiving line?

- ❀ Are there adequate rest room and cloakroom facilities?

- ❀ Will any other weddings be held in this space on our wedding day? How much breakdown time will there be between events? (Breakdown time is the time it takes to completely clean up after one event and set up for another.)

- ❀ Is there ample space for parking?

- ❀ Do you have a backup emergency generator?

- ❀ If the site is in a historic mansion or museum, how much space will be available to guests (entire building, one section or wing?) and what is off-limits? Do we need to purchase insurance in case of damage to its collection or furnishings?

When Choosing an Unusual or Outdoor Site

If you'll need to bring in a tent, equipment, or furnishings, keep these additional considerations in mind:

- Does the site provide lighting, electricity, heat, air conditioning, shelter (a tent or canopy), and kitchen facilities?

- Can the caterer work with the kitchen facilities available? If no kitchen is in sight (like in a cornfield!), can the caterer bring in a generator, cooking and refrigeration equipment, and work stations?

- What kind of access will the caterer have to service elevators and service entrances where food and equipment can be delivered and stored?

- Are there enough electrical outlets? Can the circuits carry an extra load?

- Is the site so remote (in the woods or aboard a ship) that guests will be unable to leave early if they wish?

- Has the caterer ever worked under similar conditions before?

When Erecting a Tent

- Is it waterproof? Heated? Air-conditioned?

- Does it come with windows and flooring?

- Is the floor a firm surface or soft layer of plastic covering (which high heels can sink into)? Flooring is important.

239

Natural green grass underfoot is gorgeous—unless, of course, it rained the night before, in which case it squishes underfoot and stains the hems of long dresses.

❀ Will poles and wiring be exposed? Can you decorate them?

Reception Seating

Where do we seat all these people?

A wedding reception is like any other party: A gracious host will consider where guests will be seated so that everyone feels comfortable with their dining companions.

At the ceremony, most couples stick to the traditional formula of bride's family on the left side, groom's family on the right. At the reception, any seating plan is acceptable, as long as it's sensitive to the special needs of guests. For instance, don't seat Grandma right next to the noisy band or the swinging kitchen doors, and try not to throw feuding or divorced relatives together.

Traditionally, the bridal (head) table consists of the newlyweds and their attendants. The bride and groom sit in the center, with the maid of honor next to the groom and the best man next to the bride. Spouses of the bridesmaids and ushers are seated elsewhere.

For any kind of sit-down meal, whether a buffet or served dinner, it's less chaotic if you have place cards and numbered table assignments. But this is a personal choice. Sometimes assigned seats at the rehearsal dinner but merely assigned tables at the sit-down wedding reception works just fine.

Place cards often consist of the guest's name and table number printed or written on a small card, which is sometimes then placed in an envelope. The cards are displayed on a table outside the reception room. A more informal way to do it is to post a seating chart near the door.

When planning seating, first make a floor plan of the reception room. Determine how many tables there will be and how many guests will be seated at each table. Eight to ten guests per table makes for easy conversation and prompt service.

When grouping guests, you may seat them together according to age, interests, profession, marital status, or family relationship. Be considerate of guests with special needs. Elderly guests and those with limited mobility may appreciate seats away from the band or near the buffet line.

CATERING

Catering takes the biggest bite out of the wedding budget, an average of 45 to 50 percent, so choose a caterer as carefully as you'd choose the wedding gown.

Depending on your location choice, the caterer may be an on-site banquet manager or someone you've hired from the outside to provide the food and beverages, and sometimes the table linens, china, lighting, glassware, silverware, tables, and chairs, too.

There are pros and cons to a site that provides all the services in house. While it's worry-free to have the flowers, cake, photography, music, catering, and liquor all under one roof, some couples prefer to have more personal choice over vendors. And choosing a package means you may be locked into more services than you want. (You may be paying for monogrammed matchbooks and a groom's cake whether you want those extras or not.) Keep in mind

241

that hotels will frequently charge not only tax and gratuity (called a service charge), but then tax the service charge as well.

To find a good caterer, ask friends for referrals or ask your favorite restaurant if they do off-site parties. It's a good idea to comparison shop and meet with at least three caterers. Make an appointment to discuss menus, guest-list size, and whether you prefer a buffet, sit-down dinner, or simple cocktail and hors d' oeuvres reception.

Always sample the caterer's fare! You may need to schedule this for a time when the caterer is preparing food for another event, but it's critical to ensure the food for your wedding will be delicious and attractively presented.

Karen Lucas of Blue Heron Caterers in Oakland, California, says a good caterer will want to first know where the site is, in order to gauge what kind of menu can be realistically prepared there, to determine whether there is outdoor space for dining or a buffet setup, and to see if the site has a casual or formal feel. Also pertinent will be whether the guests will be seated together in one room or spread out among other parts of the venue. "Talk to the caterer in depth," Lucas advises. "A good caterer will be able to listen to you and gather what your likes and dislikes are. It's always helpful to me to ask what restaurants the couples eat at; then I know their food preferences and price sensitivities."

A "custom" caterer is one who will work with you to tailor the menu specifically to your preferences. For instance, if the client fancies Australian prawns, the true custom caterer will move heaven and earth to get them, no matter what the cost. Or if a family tradition calls for a particular cookie to be served, the heirloom recipe will be followed and those cookies made part of the repast.

Other caterers offer set menus or packages and let you choose from a specified list of dishes, with few or no substitutions. Some caterers provide food and beverages alone, leaving it up to the couple or reception site to arrange for servers, equipment, and so on.

Choosing from a set menu has its advantages. A standard program package is often (but not always) cheaper than a custom menu, and there's no guesswork—you can be assured the caterer has those recipes down pat, having produced them time and again. On the flip side, there is little room for a personal stamp, and you run the risk of a cookie-cutter meal that has been served at dozens of other receptions.

Here's another consideration: If serving a meal, do you prefer a sit-down event or buffet? The advantage of a sit-down meal is that it's easier to control the flow of events, such as when the wedding cake is cut or the after-dinner dancing begins. The advantage to a buffet is that guests are free to mingle and circulate as they please. There's a common misconception that a buffet is always cheaper than a sit-down meal. This isn't necessarily so. With a buffet, less portion control means a caterer must prepare more food per person to keep the buffet looking full and presentable.

Food stations are also popular and encourage guests to get up and meet each other. With stations, guests sample foods cooked to order at multiple buffets featuring foods like stir-fry, kebabs, pasta and gourmet pizza, omelets, ice cream sundaes, or appetizers. Stations are festive and provide an element of entertainment, especially if something is sizzling in a wok or flambéed with a dramatic burst of flames.

Presentation is an important part of catering. How imaginatively does the caterer present and garnish foods (fresh flowers, decorative baskets, silver or lacquer trays)? What kinds of platters and serving pieces will be used? How will the servers be attired? These are all considerations.

Never choose a caterer on cost alone. A good caterer will work within your budget, even if it means paring down the whole event or choosing less expensive ingredients and food preparation techniques that require less labor.

Remember, a large part of catering costs are directly related to labor costs. Avoid foods that require carving at the table or time-consuming kitchen prep. Obviously, in-season foods cost less than out-of-season items. Generally, chicken is less expensive than beef, beef is less expensive than shellfish, and items such as imported caviar and fresh salmon, shrimp, and lobster will send any catering bill sky high. And watch out for hors d'oeuvres that have enormous variations in cost. Depending on the hors d'oeuvres you choose, the cost could be pennies apiece or several dollars each! Since guests gobble an average of five hors d'oeuvres per person per hour, the price can quickly soar.

A reputable caterer will help you determine how many guest tables are required and what size linens are needed. Generally, a 54-inch (square) card table seats four people; a 60-inch round table seats eight people; a 72-inch round table seats eight to ten; a 72-inch-long rectangular table seats six to eight; and a 96-inch rectangular table accommodates up to ten.

How About a Dance Floor?

If the reception will include dancing, you'll need about three square feet of dance floor per guest. Some hotels or sites use roll-up dance floors, or portable floors that can be laid out (in interlocking squares) in minutes. A typical dance floor setup measures approximately 24 feet by 24 feet, or 600 square feet.

245

STYLES OF TABLE SERVICE

American Service

Also called plated service, this type of table service is most commonly used in catering. Guests are seated and the food is prepared in the kitchen and served on plates carried in on large banquet trays. This is the most common and economical style, since American service allows large numbers of guests to be served quickly and requires a minimum number of servers.

French Service

Classical French service requires a "brigade de service," or six-member dining staff who prepare both hot and cold foods at tableside (and, therefore, is too expensive for most weddings). Some catering establishments, however, incorporate a few French service touches, such as carving beef to order at tableside or preparing a fresh Caesar salad or flambéed dessert. In the more common form of French service, platters of food are composed in the kitchen and taken to the table. Guests select foods, and the server, using two large silver forks, places them on each plate.

Russian Service

Foods are cooked at tableside. Servers put them on platters, present them to seated guests, and the guests serve themselves from the platters. This is sometimes also called silver service.

Buffet Service

Vegetable, main course, and dessert items are displayed on large tables along which the guests move, serving themselves. Servers usually pour beverages directly at the table. A buffet service usually requires the least amount of kitchen and wait-staff labor, but it does require more time for the overall meal.

Family Style

Guests are seated. Large platters of food are placed on the dining tables, and guests help themselves and pass the foods along the table to each other. This saves on wait-staff, but may cost you more, since the caterer can't control the portion amounts and must put full platters on the tables. (Also known as English style.)

Food Stations

This is similar to buffet service and features chefs preparing foods to order at the buffet. Stations are popularly used for serving pasta, omelets, crepes, grilled meats and fish, and ice cream sundaes or flambéed desserts.

Reception Service

Popular for cocktail parties or when only light foods or appetizers will be served. Foods are served buffet style or passed by servers. Guests stand and serve themselves.

Hand Service

A very elegant but labor-intensive style. Servers wear white gloves and each is assigned to serve only two guests. The food is prepared and plated in the kitchen, and the servers stand behind the guests until the catering captain or maître d' gives a signal, and all guests are served at precisely the same time!

TERMS YOU NEED TO KNOW

A la Carte Guests order individual items from a menu (the opposite of table d' hôte, which is a full-course, price-fixed meal).

A la Mode Usually means a dessert served with ice cream, but also refers to "in the style of" and in some places means mashed potatoes on beef!

Breakdown Time The amount of time needed to clean up after one event and completely set up for another.

Bottle Laws Term referring to the local laws for alcohol sales. For instance, in some states if you order bottles of wine for consumption at the rehearsal dinner, you may not be allowed to remove any opened bottles from the premises at the end of the party—even if they are full.

By the Bottle Liquor served and charged for by the full bottle. All bottles that have been opened must be paid for by the client.

By the Glass Liquor charged by the number of drinks served.

Cake-cutting Fee An additional fee charged for slicing and serving the wedding cake. This fee can run to $3 a person, so be sure to find out whether the caterer or site charges it!

Cash Bar A bar setup where guests pay for their own drinks. A cash bar is the opposite of an open bar (where drinks are paid for by the party hosts).

Corkage Fee Fee charged to open and serve drinks you bring in from outside the hotel or catering establishment. Includes the cost of labor, ice, mixers, and so on.

Gratuity A service charge added to the food and liquor bill. Usually runs between 15 to 20 percent of the total food and liquor costs.

Guarantee The minimum number of servings to be paid for by the client. (Which means if you guarantee fifty guests and only twenty show up, you are still paying for the fifty-person "guarantee.")

House Brand The wine or liquor served when you don't specify a particular brand. (Ask what they'll be pouring; the house brand is usually offered at a more reasonable price but may not be up to your standard.)

Specialty Brand A particular brand of wine or liquor specified by the client.

Plus, Plus Means gratuities and any special taxes added to the prices charged for food and drinks.

Skirting The ruffled or pleated draping used to decorate buffet and head tables. Ask if there is an extra charge for this.

QUESTIONS TO ASK THE CATERER

- How long have you been in business? Where did you receive your culinary training?
- Do you work from a set menu or package, or can we request a menu tailored to our preferences?
- What kind of health permit and liability insurance do you carry?
- Are you licensed to serve liquor?
- Can you provide other services such as flowers, table linens, candles, chairs, tables, dance floor, runners, candelabras, canopy, or chuppah?
- Is the cost of the service staff included in the price?

❀ If not, how many waiters/waitresses will be needed, and what is the charge per hour? Overtime charges? When do overtime charges kick in?

❀ How will the servers be attired?

❀ Will the caterer I've hired be present at the reception on the wedding day to oversee things and make sure all goes smoothly?

❀ Are all charges clearly stated in the contract? (This includes types of foods, amounts, number of guests, complete menu listing, per-person charge, liquor charges, setup charges, and equipment charges.)

❀ Do you require a guaranteed number of guests?

❀ When is the deposit due to hold the date? When is the balance due?

❀ When is the final guest count due? What if we have unexpected guests show up? Can you accommodate them? What will the additional charge be?

❀ Is the caterer charged an extra fee or percentage by the reception site? Is this extra fee included in our price?

❀ Have you ever catered a wedding reception before at the site we've chosen?

❀ Are there extra fees for cake-cutting, corkage, linens, rental of furniture or serving pieces, mandatory gratuity, setup or production charges, bar setup, mixers?

❀ Will you provide special dietary meals upon request?

- ⊕ Do you handle the cleanup and rental returns?

 ⊕ Can we supply our own liquor?

- ⊕ How are drink costs calculated? Is there a refund for unopened bottles of liquor? What brands will be served?

- ⊕ Do you supply plates, glasses, silverware, and linens?

- ⊕ Do you provide the wedding cake?

- ⊕ Do you provide the flowers?

- ⊕ Will you prepare an heirloom family recipe (such as a cookie or wedding-cake recipe) for us on request?

- ⊕ What are the breakage fees for china, glassware, and so on?

- ⊕ What is your cancellation policy? Are any deposits refundable?

- ⊕ How many servers will be required for a wedding of this size (including bartenders, waiters, valet parking, cloakroom attendants, security, and so on)?

WAYS TO TRIM CATERING AND RECEPTION COSTS

- ⊕ Look for a cost-free or nearly free reception site such as a private home, church hall, or public community center or club. Often members of a club, theater, or aquarium pay lower fees than non-members do.

- ⊕ Book the site for a time least in demand for weddings, such as off-peak wedding months (January through March), one or two days before Christmas, or midweek.

- ⊕ Use homegrown or in-season flowers, or rent potted plants.

251

- Ask the baker to create edible centerpieces (such as fruit baskets or flower-shaped cakes).

- Plan the reception for a time when you aren't expected to serve a full meal, such as midafternoon (when hors d'oeuvres and punch would be appropriate), or late evening, when guests will be impressed by a showstopping wedding cake and champagne toast.

- Balloon decorations tend to be less pricey than fresh flowers. Or let the flowers do double duty at both the ceremony and reception. (Assign someone you trust to transport them to the reception, right after the ceremony.)

- Limit the reception to three hours, instead of the usual four or five.

- Choose "house" brands of wine, liquor, and soda.

- Hire a photographer to work for a limited number of hours at the reception or ceremony, and ask friends and family to fill in the rest.

- Skip the cocktail hour or open bar—both add precipitously to the cost.

- Serve champagne with the wedding cake only, and not during the reception.

- Don't even *think* about serving a fresh-seafood bar.

- Borrow, rather than rent, serving pieces or furniture items such as chafing dishes, candelabras, folding chairs, or platters.

- Order only main dishes from the caterer. Some caterers will allow you to do this if you're having the reception at a home. Ask family and friends to fill in the rest—breads, liquor, soft drinks, salads, appetizers, and so on.

- ❀ Pare down the guest list.

- ❀ Cut everywhere possible. Trimming just one item from the menu, like a fruit cup or tomato juice, can save a lot when multiplied by two hundred guests. Forgo party favors, or make them yourself.

- ❀ Use the bridal bouquet and attendants' bouquets as center-pieces on the head table at the reception.

- ❀ Serve the wedding cake as the dessert.

253

Chapter Fifteen

The Honeymoon

We're off, alone at last!

Traditionally, the honeymoon has marked the first time the couple was alone together and the time for the official consummation of the marriage.

These days, a honeymoon is considered more of a romantic getaway vacation and a special chance for newlyweds to devote time only to each other, away from the demands of work and the "real" world.

Most couples leave honeymoon planning until the end when the budget has dwindled and their travel options are slim. But even if resources and time are limited, plan to take some sort of a honeymoon. It is a welcome respite after all the commotion of planning a wedding, and since marriage is a major transition, even a few days alone together will help you begin the adjustment to a shared life. (Besides, how often in your life will you get the chance to be totally oblivious to the outside world?)

According to traditional wedding etiquette, it's up to the groom to plan the honeymoon. The bride can help by suggesting possible destinations or making phone calls to travel agents.

One Florida groom did the planning with grand style. He tantalized his future wife with promises of a surprise destination and the single clue: Pack for two climates. He took her to Hawaii for one week and Alaska for another!

256

"We had a destination wedding at a country inn in Manchester, Vermont. Many of our guests came for the wedding and stayed at that inn or at nearby hotels. My funniest memory is of the innkeeper kissing a spouting fish in a fountain there—it was how he got the fountain to get unclogged! But he didn't realize all one hundred wedding guests were watching him as he did it. It was really hysterical. Just as I was ready to head down the inn stairs and sweep out through the back garden over a bridge to the guests waiting outside, it started to pour rain! It had been sunny till the moment before. So I walked down to the bottom of the stairs and everyone had assembled in the living room for the ceremony. Then, the moment the ceremony ended, the sky was clear again."

—Andrea Eginton Seton, Vermont September bride

WHERE WILL YOU GO?

Tropical destinations like Tahiti and Hawaii are romantic favorites among honeymooners (picture waterfalls and vivid sunsets), but any locale can be perfect, even if it's just miles from home. Don't feel pressured to book a faraway trip just because you think everyone else does. Consider the following popular destinations:

- The Hawaiian Islands
- Disneyland (California) or Disneyworld (Florida)
- New York City
- The Florida Keys
- California wine country
- Las Vegas
- Yosemite National Park
- Maine
- Hilton Head Island, South Carolina
- The Cayman Islands (a trio of Caribbean islands about 500 miles southwest of Florida)
- The Dutch Caribbean Islands (located off the coast of Venezuela)

- Tahiti
- The Greek islands, especially Santorini
- Cancun, Mexico
- Bermuda
- Paris
- London
- Majorca
- The Bahamas
- The U.S. Virgin Islands

If traveling a long distance, think about giving yourself a day to recuperate from the wedding before hopping on a plane or train. These days, it's not uncommon for couples to spend their first married night at a local hotel and then gather with out-of-town wedding guests the next day for a brunch or final farewell. And since many couples have lived together, or host and pay for their weddings themselves, they don't feel pressured to formally "depart" the wedding before everyone else in order to make a grand getaway. They also want to stay and enjoy the party till the very end.

Think carefully about what kind of trip you'll *both* enjoy. Do you want to be active (hiking, snorkeling, exploring historic ruins) or more passive (lolling on a beach, reading a good book)? Do you want to dress up for dinner each night or go casual?

All too often, one of the newlyweds books a secluded beach holiday thinking it's the ultimate romantic experience, only to find their mate gets sun poisoned easily or goes stir-crazy after a day of staring at the waves.

Did You Know . . . ?

Here in the States, Minnie and Mickey Mouse can help you plan a honeymoon/wedding with storybook appeal. Disneyworld in Florida has a team of specialists to help couples plan events with as much or as little Disney fantasy as they desire. You can choose anything from an elegant, traditional wedding and honeymoon to a themed wedding in which the bride arrives in Cinderella's glass coach or accompanied by costumed characters.

THE DESTINATION WEDDING AND HONEYMOON

Today's couples are setting aside more money for the honeymoon and making their stays longer, an average of ten to fourteen days, wedding experts say. Many couples are older, more sophisticated, and more well traveled than in past generations. With their dual incomes and travel savvy, they don't always want the standard island resort overrun with everyone else who just tied the knot, too.

Creative Leisure International in Petaluma, California, is among a growing number of travel operators specializing in destination weddings, in which the couple exchange vows in an unusual or romantic corner of the world and remain there for the honeymoon. Often the bride and groom invite their families and friends to join them—and the wedding becomes something of a three- or four-day family reunion, with scheduled parties and events.

Travel companies and wedding consultants versed in destination weddings, like fairy godmothers, take care of all the logistical, legal, and travel considerations for you, including tickets, accommodations, and the documents and certificates needed to marry in a foreign locale.

A destination-wedding specialist handles all the pesky details (like finding local translators, caterers, witnesses, and florists) and knows the scoop on how long a waiting period is required to marry in that country or what currency is accepted for payment of fees. For example, until recently you could pay for a marriage license in Antigua only by using local postage stamps.

Among the most popular sites for destination honeymoon/weddings are the Greek Isles, Hawaii, Central America, and Africa. International Ventures, based in Wilton, Connecticut, specializes in honeymoon weddings in Africa.

259

Imagine arriving by chartered plane to your own private remote camp on the African Serengeti Plain for a luxury safari honeymoon for two! International Ventures will also organize custom scuba safaris, camel safaris, and horseback-riding or bird-watching honeymoon expeditions.

Destination Details

Keep in mind that regulations on getting married abroad vary from state to state, and in some foreign countries there may be waiting periods of months or days. Don't leave the red tape till the last minute. Some countries require translations of documents notarized by their consulate in the United States in advance, with separate documentation if also planning a religious ceremony.

If you are considering a foreign locale, begin by contacting the government tourist office or consulate. Be sure to double-check the information you receive and complete the paperwork and necessary documents several months in advance. Keep records of with whom you have spoken or corresponded, along with the date and time. Double-check all the arrangements a week before leaving the country. If traveling to a spot known for political unrest, check with the U.S. Passport Agency or State Department for travel advisories before departing.

Ask the travel or wedding consultant, consulate, or resort manager these important questions before marrying abroad:

- ❀ Can Americans legally marry in that country?
- ❀ Are there medical, residency, or blood test requirements? Residency may mean residing in that country for months prior to the wedding, or just days.
- ❀ What documents are required?

- Is there a waiting period between obtaining the marriage license and the actual wedding date?

- Must banns, the proclamation of intent to marry, be posted in the church?

- Must they be notarized? Are there any documents that must be sent to the foreign country in advance? Must you present them in person abroad?

- Do you need the services of a lawyer abroad?

- Will you have access to a translator?

- What kinds of fees are required? What form of payment is necessary?

261

MAKING RESERVATIONS

For best rates, book a honeymoon at least three to six months in advance. Expect to spend anywhere from $800 for a weekend getaway for two to $5,000 or more for an extended vacation. For help in planning, consider using the services of a travel agent. Friends and relatives will offer endless suggestions ("You'll *love* the Canary Islands!") but a travel professional can help you choose a destination to fit your personal interests, budget, and time constraints. And a travel agent will keep you advised of the best airfares and hotel rates.

Most travel agency services are free, because travel agents are paid directly by travel suppliers, according to the American Society of Travel Agents (see appendix). Travel agents can arrange for the following special services:

- all types of domestic and international air travel

- hotel and resort accommodations

- tour packages

- ground transportation (getting from the airport or train station to your hotel or another connecting flight)

- car rental

- assistance with special foreign travel requirements or documents (Do I need vaccinations? Are there State Department advisories against traveling to some pockets of the globe? Do I need to bring my marriage certificate or proof of citizenship?)

- assistance with insurance protection, passport, and visa applications

- advice on the local climate, local attractions, and what to pack.

When traveling abroad, allow at least three months to arrange for a passport. You may need to locate an original copy of your birth certificate, which can take weeks, and allow for processing of the passport photo and papers. In case of emergencies, the State Department can arrange for speedier processing at some offices, but you may have to bring proof of travel arrangements, such as an airline ticket for imminent travel.

A trained travel professional can also help you sort the travel bargains from the rip-offs. Think about it: Journeys involve services that can't be inspected before payment is made. You may have only a glossy brochure to go on (which usually showcases the hotel or resort in the best possible light). It isn't always easy to determine whether the "deluxe" hotel is really deluxe (or a dump) or to evaluate all the restrictions, special conditions, and fine print that can add substantially to the price.

Many travel bargains are legitimate. Hotel rates and airfares tend to plummet during off-seasons, and travel suppliers would rather offer reduced rates than have unoccupied rooms. But to avoid being taken, keep the following advisories from ASTA's *Avoiding Travel Problems* brochure in mind:

❀ Does the price seem unbelievably low? If it sounds too good to be true, it probably is.

❀ If you get an unsolicited phone call from someone offering a travel bargain or claiming you've won a trip, be wary! Never give your credit card number over the phone to a person or company with whom you aren't familiar.

❀ Be wary if the solicitor is unwilling to give his or her full name and the company name, street address, and phone number. Don't give in to immediate pressure over the phone.

❀ Ask if the company has an escrow account—and in what name, and at which bank.

❀ Hang up if the company is unwilling to send you written information about the offer (including cost, specific terms, and conditions) before you commit any money.

❀ Don't accept vague descriptions such as "all major hotels" or "major airlines." If the travel or hotel reservations are booked through another company, ask for the name, address, and phone number of that company.

263

✷ Are you quoted one price, then asked to provide an additional deposit, purchase another ticket, or pay a fee to join a club or cover processing costs? Don't stand for it!

Time-share resorts

Some resort vacation offers are made by companies trying to sell time-share options on condominiums. A time-share means a buyer purchases the use of the condominium or villa for a specific limited amount of time each year, say a week or two. Ask whether the vacation time will be spent inspecting any properties and whether you must pay a fee should you choose not to purchase the time-share.

THE ALL-INCLUSIVE VACATION

While some travelers love the freedom of choosing their services à la carte (booking the plane tickets, hotel, and meals on their own), others prefer the ease of purchasing a honeymoon package.

A travel package is usually paid for in advance and includes the hotel accommodations, airfare, meals, and airport transfers. Some all-inclusive resorts also include sports instruction and equipment, court fees, drinks, nightly entertainment, excursions, and even tips. With a true all-inclusive vacation, the only extra expenses you'll have are things like film and souvenirs. An all-inclusive vacation can be a bargain and a worry-free way to travel, since so few expenses crop up.

The Cruise

Cruises rank among the most popular all-inclusive vacations. Once aboard, the fare includes a cabin, all daytime and evening entertainment, and all meals.

Cruise vacations can suit every budget, and they last anywhere from three days to several months. Ships offer a remarkable range of onboard services, from hair salons to spas, movie theaters, pools, nightclubs, casinos, golf driving, skeet shooting, and aerobics.

In the past, cruise ships were generally segregated into first-, second-, or third-class sections, with travelers restricted to only those areas of the ship for which they'd paid. Today's cruise ships are "one-class," which means everyone on board can use all of the ship's facilities. The price of a stateroom is based primarily on its size and location. Generally, the higher the deck is above the waterline, the pricier the cabin. First-time cruise passengers are sometimes disappointed that their cabin seems postage-stamp-size, since cruise accommodations are usually smaller than the average hotel room. Often the beds fold down from the ceiling. Don't fret; most people on a cruise spend their time wandering around deck enjoying the round-the-clock activities. And don't be frightened when the cruise activities begin with a lifeboat drill; it's standard procedure so that everyone knows what to do in the rare case of emergency at sea.

PACKING TIPS

⊛ Mark luggage inside and outside with name and address. If no one will be at home to receive misdirected luggage, use your company address and phone number.

⊛ Make two copies of important travel documents, including passport, visa, itinerary, personal identification, and numbers to call in case credit cards are lost or stolen. Leave one copy at home (in case your suitcase with the copy gets lost too). Don't bring along any more credit cards than you need.

⊛ If your luggage is lost or misdirected, report it immediately. If you wait too long to report it or forget to claim it, the luggage may be sent to the airline's regional unclaimed luggage department in another part of the country.

⊛ Keep a list of traveler's-check serial numbers, denominations, and where you purchased them, plus the number to call in case of loss or theft. Leave a copy of the information with a friend or relative who will be easy to reach day or night in case of emergency.

⊛ Pack a carry-on bag with a change of clothing and toilet articles in case your checked luggage is misplaced.

- Pack any valuables, medication, or important papers in your carry-on bag.

- Carry prescription medications in the original container! Begin any prescription medications before leaving home, in case of allergic reactions. Those with a medical condition should bring along their doctor's name, phone number, fax number, and address.

- Pack an extra pair of prescription glasses or contact lenses.

- Retain baggage-claim checks after checking luggage.

- Ask a friend or relative to housesit for you and collect the mail or feed a pet while you are away.

- Never leave your luggage unattended or trust it to someone you don't know. Notify security if anyone asks you to carry packages or luggage on board for them.

- Plan to check in at the airport at least one hour prior to a domestic flight; two hours before an international flight.

- Find out about customs restrictions before departing on an international flight.

- Confirm your reservations by phone before departing, especially in peak travel seasons around major holidays when airlines sometimes overbook.

- Pack rubber-soled shoes or deck shoes for traction on cruise-ship decks and stairs, which may be damp from sea mist.

- Check out the airline's policy for refunds and lost luggage. Find out what compensation is available for passengers who are "bumped." Since airlines sometimes overbook flights to compensate for no-shows, travelers may be voluntarily or involuntarily bumped, even if they have reservations! In case of an overbooked flight, most airlines will ask for volunteers to give up their seats in exchange for a free round-trip ticket and the promise of a confirmed seat on the next available flight. If involuntarily bumped, however, you may be eligible for the free ticket, plus cash compensation. By investigating the airline's bumping policy beforehand, you'll be in the best position to negotiate for the full compensation allowed.

In Case Problems Arise

Did your travel agency close overnight, leaving you stranded without tickets? Were the hotel services downright awful? If travel problems occur, try settling it amicably at the source. For instance, a hotel manager will want to know about poor service and may offer you a reduced rate or extra services like meals to compensate.

If that doesn't work, keep copies of all receipts and report any problems to the local Better Business Bureau, state attorney general's office, state consumer affairs department, or the American Society of Travel Agents Consumer Affairs Department.

When making phone calls to report a problem, keep a log of dates, times, and with whom you spoke.

From Here to Matrimony

Wedding Stress, Preparation for Marriage, and How to Handle It All

"If this is the happiest time of my life, why am I so miserable?"

Even when couples have the luxury of a long engagement to plan a wedding, the common complaint is often "So much to do; so little time!"

Finding the perfect dress, ironing out the seating arrangements, mediating family squabbles, and trying to juggle it all while performing at work can be a piece of cake—or a recipe for major anxiety. It's no wonder engaged couples find themselves wondering why they're stressed out when they're supposed to be ecstatic.

Normal? You bet. According to a *Modern Bride* survey (Jan. 1993), 80 percent of engaged women reported increased stress since their engagement, and nearly half (48 percent) entertained thoughts about canceling the wedding and eloping.

Feeling stressed out is more the rule than the exception, it seems. And no wonder. Getting married is more than just a walk down the aisle; it's an enormously emotional proposition that psychologists rank high up among the top ten anxiety-producing life changes like death, divorce, or losing a job.

Think about it. Marriage represents both a new beginning and union and the loss of some level of individuality. It results in the total reshifting of all the boundaries that make up the family system—a sort of reshuffling of all the cards in your life.

This is the time when couples realize just how connected they are to their "families of origin" (your mom, dad, siblings, and close relatives) and yet how independent they are. Sure, your mother has always insisted that wedding receptions mean a big reception and sit-down dinner; it doesn't mean *you* have to buy into that.

When Marie Rienzo of New Jersey was married forty-three years ago, her sister and two brothers felt her marriage had "broken up the set." In a healthy and necessary way, it had. She married, moved out, and established her own family, and her parents and siblings were affected by that change too. Things haven't really changed much since then.

Some family therapists call this process "differentiation," which is a fancy term for learning to be a self-reliant individual establishing an intimate relationship with a partner, while also remaining an involved member of an extended family. (No wonder you're tired; you're renegotiating the parameters of multiple relationships when you marry.)

Among the most common wedding stressors are financial worries (How can we pay for all this?), job pressures, not having enough time to do it all, planning a long-distance wedding, planning an interfaith wedding, or trying to please everyone.

Many couples today are paying for their own weddings, and when parents offer to "chip in," things can get sticky. Suddenly it's not their wedding, it's Mom's. And brides don't always know when to step in and assert themselves— and when they do, hurt feelings can result.

The way to prevent stress overload is through careful organization and planning. Hire a consultant. Delegate tasks. Don't do it all yourself. Decide who will be in charge of what, and when. Literally schedule some time for relaxation and for *not* worrying about the wedding. Learn to negotiate and compromise. Take a break between overcoming major hurdles. For example, book the reception hall and caterer; then take a few weeks off before calling florists or photographers.

"One of the biggest problems couples have is going into this without thinking of a realistic budget," said Annena Sorenson of tie The Knot in Palo Alto, California. "They don't realize that a wedding is an overwhelming project, a major event to plan, and most people don't have any experience in planning major events. It is also the event closest to the heart."

Stress management experts suggest determining whether an issue is a "ten-dollar" or a "ten-cent" problem. Are you willing to expend a lot of your time worrying about it, or a just a little? Some problems warrant ten dollars' worth of aggravation; others don't. Worrying about whether the gown will arrive in time is a ten-dollar problem; deciding what hors d'oeuvres to feed the band is a ten-cent problem.

Tips for Stress-free Planning

- ❀ Consider hiring a professional consultant to keep track of the billion details for you.
- ❀ Keep up with writing thank-you notes.
- ❀ To cut down on confusion, don't try to interview more than three vendors in each category (flowers, photographer, consultants, bakers, and so on).
- ❀ Keep a loose-leaf notebook with vendor contracts, notes, swatches, and magazine clippings.
- ❀ Prepare yourself mentally and spiritually. Set aside special time during wedding planning to work on your loving relationship, not on the wedding itself.
- ❀ Eat a healthful diet and get plenty of rest.
- ❀ Remember the three C's: compromise, communicate, and be considerate.
- ❀ Stick to your budget to avoid a postwedding letdown.

PREPARATION FOR MARRIAGE

Are you ready? Really ready? That is, are you prepared for a wedding day and for all the happily ever after years?

In many ways, organizing a wedding is a training manual for married life. Huh?

Couples learn to negotiate, compromise, squabble, celebrate, stand their ground, have fun together, work for a common goal, and explore shared ideals. (And you thought you were just picking out party favors.) Arguing over where Aunt Rose sits at the reception or whether you really need a cake with gold leaf is a valuable experience, because you're learning about each other's family traditions and setting the watermark for standards you'll both share.

There is no secret formula for a happy marriage. (Sorry.) Marriages flourish or flounder for reasons personal and specific to the husband and wife. But family therapists generally agree that certain family systems "work" because the family members work at their relationship. All couples are family systems, regardless of whether they have children or not.

Don't fall prey to the common myths about marriage—things like "We were always meant for each other" or "Love conquers all." Another one is "Love doesn't change." Nonsense. Life is all about change. Enduring love is not the same as romantic, passionate love experienced in the first days or months of a relationship. One of my Fairfield University graduate-school professors once said, "Couples can't remain in that red-hot stage of love forever, or they'd simply burn up!"

273

Which is not to say that passion has to die or sexual interest must slump. Simply that as couples go through different stages of life, they move from an idealized view of their partner to a more realistic view (warts and all), to a resolution stage where they accept and celebrate the person for who he is (as in, "He may be no Fabio, but he's not a total jerk, and I love him").

In my work with engaged and married couples, I've noticed another love myth that gets people into trouble: "If you really loved me, you would know what I want." Remember Laura Petrie saying this to husband Rob in the *Dick Van Dyke* TV show? How can anyone expect his spouse to be a mind reader? For instance, how could she know that you've always wanted a homemade birthday cake and surprise party if you've never told her?

All the different schools of psychology and marriage therapy have their own models of what constitutes a healthy family and what makes marriage work. In general, loving couples have many of the following qualities:

Sense of Commitment Both partners are in it for the long haul and willing to work through tough times. Doing something positive each day of your marriage to enhance your relationship is like money in the bank.

Dreams! Loving couples have images of what they would like to become and expectations for each other. They take responsibility for changing their own lives.

Positive World View The world is seen as full of possibilities, and satisfaction is expected from interpersonal relationships.

Family Customs and Traditions Successful couples perpetuate customs and traditions and want to pass them on to their children.

Intimacy Loving couples have an active, satisfying sex life and aren't afraid to demonstrate warmth and affection.

Hierarchy When children arrive, loving couples work as a parenting team. There is a clear chain of command so that everyone knows what the family rules are and who makes them.

Conflict Management Loving couples handle conflict through resolution and compromise. They know that flexibility is a real strength.

Time Spent Together Loving couples make time for shared activities and for each other. Make a point of making "dates" with your spouse throughout the married years.

Clear Communication They say what they think and feel, share feelings of hurt and anger, and accept the feelings of others.

Altruistic Loving couples see themselves as part of a larger community. They are generous and reach out to help others.

Crisis Management Crises are seen not as disasters but as opportunities for growth and change.

Sense of Humor! Healthy families know how to laugh and see the positive side of even bleak situations.

Doing Your Preparation Homework

Some religious groups require engaged couples to undergo premarital programs. In the Catholic Church, these programs are called Pre-Cana preparation. It is also possible to find secular premarital training programs offered through universities or continuing-education programs. It makes sense to take time for working on your relationship. After all, people take time to shop for a new car, prepare for a career, or buy a house, don't they? Marriage preparation programs can be particularly valuable, and topics often include: financial planning, family planning, goal setting, conflict resolution, and communication techniques.

The PAIRS (Practical Application of Intimate Relationship Skills) Foundation (see appendix), for example, offers programs for couples, singles, marriage and family therapists, and mental health professionals that concentrate on practical everyday skills for "divorce prevention," including communication, bonding, conflict resolution, sexuality, and appreciating each other's unique personality.

The Prepare and Enrich Program (see appendix), a counseling tool used by more than 25,000 counselors nationwide, arranges for couples to meet with a trained counselor and individually take a scientifically designed questionnaire that identifies their strengths and weaknesses as a couple. It also summarizes how each views the relationship. Then they meet with the counselor for a feedback session. This kind of program is enormously valuable. It helps couples get their marriage off to a good start, build on the strengths they have, and pinpoint areas of their relationship that might be problematic or in need of enrichment.

Got Cold Feet?

Couples with persistent doubts about marriage or their choice of a future spouse are wise to take advantage of specialized training or seek help from a therapist. Many therapists do premarital sessions.

It's reasonable to get cold feet briefly before a wedding. After all, this is an enormous step, and couples worry about whether they're doing the right thing, whether their spouse will change, or whether they can possibly love one person their whole life long. But truly nagging doubts that don't go away and only intensify as the wedding approaches should be addressed.

SPECIAL SITUATIONS

Must a Bride Change Her Name?

No way. While it was once obligatory for the bride to take her husband's surname as her own, that custom is no longer the standard.

For personal or professional reasons, many women choose to keep their maiden names their whole life—and it's perfectly legal. The name-change issue is a difficult one, and some women are reluctant to completely give up the name they have carried since birth. In that case, consider the following options:

Keep one name for business, the other for social situations and everyday life.

Combine the two names, either with a hyphen (Mary Smith-Jones) or without (Mary Smith Jones). Before you do, think carefully about the resulting hybrid. Audiences howled with laughter when Murphy Brown's Corky Sherwood became Corky Sherwood Forest.

Some women use their husband's name only after they have children. Decide whose name (both? hers? his?) the children will have. Keep in mind that when Junior goes to school, some teachers mistakenly assume that parents with different last names are divorced. And it can be confusing for a young child to wonder why Mom's last name is different from his and Dad's.

277

Avoid awkward social situations by introducing yourself properly: "Hi, I'm Madeline Barillo, Alexandra Flagg's mother [or Greg Flagg's wife]."

Some couples merge their two names to form a completely new one: Ann Grant and Mark Love may become the Grantloves. This kind of name change must be done legally.

Use your maiden name as your middle name.

A new bride who plans to take her husband's name should notify Social Security. Failure to report the change is a frequent cause of errors in wage records and may affect the amount of benefits a person is eligible for at retirement. (The same applies to a woman who divorces and resumes using her maiden name.) You'll also want to notify the Internal Revenue Service of the name change, and any change of address.

And remember to adjust the following as well: bank records, will, credit cards, insurance policies, automobile records (insurance, registration, driver's license), telephone company, deeds or property titles, employee or school identification cards, magazine subscriptions, passport, pension plan, voter registration card.

It's a good idea to keep a separate credit line in your name, as well as a joint credit line with your spouse.

No Matter How Hard I Try, My In-Laws Don't Like Me

This can be a painful situation, especially if your future spouse is unsympathetic. Everyone wants to feel loved and accepted when becoming part of a larger, extended family. Unfortunately, it isn't always possible to be valued and appreciated by a fiancé's family.

There could be any number of reasons: They haven't taken the time to get to really know you, they wanted their son to marry the girl next door, or they're afraid your marital relationship will affect their special bond with their son or daughter. Parents who have overly invested in their children often have a hard time letting go and are threatened by a son- or-daughter-in-law.

Take the time to express your concerns openly with your future spouse. Don't take your anger or anxiety out on him. Resist the urge to force him to take sides. (They've been his parents a lot longer than he has been your fiancé.) It may be awkward or difficult at first, but make a warm overture to your in-laws expressing your common love for their child: "It's very important to me to develop a warm, respectful relationship with you. We both love your son very much and want the best for him."

Give it time. If all else fails, and your in-laws always remain frosty, think carefully about why their approval matters. As long as their hostile feelings don't jeopardize your marriage, it may be possible to simply accept it and move on. If in-law problems cause a real rift, it's time to seek marital counseling.

Should a Pregnant Bride Have a Real Wedding?

Sometimes a pregnancy speeds up wedding plans a bit. A pregnant bride has every right to the wedding she always dreamed of—big reception, long white gown, whatever.

In the past, couples who were expecting a baby before marriage tradition-ally married quickly and without much fanfare. Times have changed. The bride and groom have every right to invite their friends and celebrate the way they please. One Vermont couple who were overjoyed at the news of the bride's

279

pregnancy decided to marry in a small private ceremony before the baby was born and later hold a "real" wedding reception after their child had arrived. Bride, groom, and baby posed for the wedding pictures.

Bear in mind that some guests may still be uncomfortable at the sight of a pregnant woman in a wedding dress and may openly express their shock or displeasure.

Decide how the two of you would like to handle the situation—whether it's keeping the pregnancy a private issue or sharing the news. Most couples will want to tell the officiant and also inform the bridal shop retailer (who can help you choose a flattering gown that will still fit properly by the time of the wedding).

If the pregnancy is the *only* reason you are marrying, think very carefully about whether it's a good enough reason. Marriages are built on trust, respect, shared values and goals, and of course love. Children tend to suffer if their parents are suffering, so think twice about your future happiness.

His Kids Hate Mine and Mine Hate His

A remarriage often means carrying extra baggage—the scars of a previous relationship, worries about the future, and one—or even two—sets of children. That also means a possible four sets of grandparents and two ex-spouses. (And you thought this marriage was just the two of you.)

These days, family therapists refer to the "blended" family to describe this extended family formed by remarriage. Becoming a blended family takes time—often years—and all sorts of allegiances, disappointments, turf wars, and new roles need to be worked out. The advantage of a remarriage is that one can learn from previous mistakes in a relationship and strive to build a better one. Also, people going into second marriages tend to be older and more financially secure.

On the flip side, there may be financial obligations to a previous spouse, as well as emotional ties and unresolved conflicts. An uncomfortable triangle often forms between the person who has recently remarried and is still trying to "co-parent" with an ex-husband or ex-wife.

Few blended families function as blissfully as TV's Brady bunch. When a parent has been single for a long time, he often forms a tight bond with his own children in order to pull through a traumatic divorce situation. When a new mate comes along, the children invariably feel rejected and threatened, say family therapists, and may express those feelings in anger toward the new spouse (the interloper). Everyone has to renegotiate his role in the family system. Add another set of kids to the picture, and loyalties and ties must be juggled once more.

Don't expect to become a loving, tight family overnight. Mental health professionals often advise couples to set aside special time each day for their own children, to remind them that even though a marriage has taken place, their love for their child will never diminish.

During the earliest stages of the marriage, it's a good idea for each parent to discipline his own children. Gradually, everyone will feel comfortable enough to express themselves and stand their ground.

Involving children in the wedding reinforces the idea of a unified new family, right from the start. This can be done by including the child in the wedding party or assigning him a special task (handing out programs, reading the liturgy, standing next to you at the altar, giving the parent away). Some couples invite their children to stand next to them during the vows and ring exchange. Others honor their children with a special family medallion, a silver necklace placed around the child's neck as a pledge of unending love (see chapter 12 on ceremonies).

How to Cope with the World Butting In

Ever since we got engaged, people keep asking personal questions: "Why aren't his parents chipping in for wedding expenses?" "Why not just live together?" "How can you afford a down payment on a house?" Help! How can we handle this?

When couples announce an engagement, their private relationship suddenly seems so public. Friends, loved ones, and even acquaintances feel inclined to voice their opinions on every facet of wedding planning and expect the bride or groom to gracefully sit back and take it all in.

When feeling that personal boundaries are being trod upon, don't simmer—say something! A simple "We haven't decided on that" or "That is a very personal matter" should suffice.

You can always turn the embarrassing question around by saying, "Yes, Jim's parents are not helping us with wedding expenses. Would *you* like to?"

How Do I Handle My Parents' Unhappiness that I'm Marrying a Much Older Person?

Think about it. Most couples marry someone with similar interests, values, and education—which usually means someone close in age. Yet it's not uncommon to find older men marrying younger women (or older women marrying younger men).

When a future spouse is a contemporary of your parents, it may be awkward for everyone. The future spouse may already have children close to your own age. Your parents' objections may include worries over whether you will produce grandchildren and anxieties over the older spouse's future health. (Obviously, a thirty-year-old who marries a sixty-year-old has a greater chance of becoming a young widow or widower than if she or he married someone closer to her or his age.) If your future spouse has children, your parents may feel you've been "saddled" with parenting chores. And there is the possibility that one of you will be ready to retire when the other is just hitting stride in a career.

When a young man marries an older woman, there is the chance that the couple will never have children, simply because a woman's biological clock runs out before a man's. Men can father children well into their elderly years, but women's childbearing years usually halt by midlife.

If faced with objections from loved ones about your spouse's age, take the time to explain why you were attracted to this person and why you feel committed enough to marry. Sometimes a parent's reassurance that your love is real and deep will erase any anxieties. After all, love has no age limit.

As a Gay Couple, We Want to Announce Our Bond in a Marriage Ceremony. Where Do We Start?

There's no traditional etiquette to fall back on here for guidance, since gay marriages haven't been part of mainstream society. Begin by finding out whether your state legally recognizes the union of two people of the same sex in a marriage. As far as I know, most religions don't. Some states already have laws that now make it possible for a longtime companion to legally "inherit" a rent-controlled apartment, a right formerly reserved for only a legal spouse. Also consider writing your own ceremony and including passages that are meaningful to both of you.

My Fiancée Insists on a Prenuptial Agreement.
Doesn't She Trust Me?

Financial planners often quip that "nobody plans to fail, they just fail to plan."

A prenuptial agreement is a legal form of protection against a bad marital outcome. Everyone hopes for a lifelong marriage, but unfortunately divorces happen. Today, both the bride and groom often enter into marriage with established assets they've worked hard for and want to hold onto if things go sour. A prenuptial agreement is a legal way to safeguard things like pension savings, property, trust funds, money you've brought to the marriage, children's college funds, an expected inheritance, personal valuables, or family heirlooms.

If you decide to have a prenuptial agreement, it should be drawn up well before the wedding, allowing enough time for the bride's lawyer and the groom's lawyer to negotiate the details and hammer out a mutually satisfactory outcome. It must be witnessed.

We've *Had* It! We Can't Stand Another Minute of Details and
Wedding Stress. How Can We Elope?

Just do it! Elopements were common in 18th-century British novels, where the underage heroine had to travel to Gretna Green, Scotland, to get married. Today couples elope for any number of reasons. They may be older, or marrying again, and simply don't want the commotion and expense of a big-deal wedding. They may be marrying against the wishes of loved ones or just want the romance and adventure of picking up and getting married on the spot.

Shannon Smith of Illinois eloped with her fiancé to a quaint country inn in Connecticut. Her parents knew all about it beforehand and gave their blessing. "We both wanted to do it," she recalled. "When it came down to it, we didn't want the hassles, the big expense of a large wedding. We just wanted to enjoy our time together." Shannon comes from a long line of elopers. Her mother had eloped, and so had her grandmother, her brother, and relatives of her stepfather.

When considering elopement, think about the effect it will have on your friends and relatives. They may feel cheated out of a wedding, bereft and excluded. Also, examine whether the choice is based on your parents' disapproval of the marriage. Think carefully about why they don't approve and whether the reasons are valid.

We Aren't Even Married Yet, and Both Sets of Parents Are Squabbling over Who "Gets" Us for Thanksgiving and Who "Gets" Us for Christmas

Welcome to couplehood! Suddenly, you can't accept a kindly invitation to her or his parent's house for the holidays without offending your own parents.

Get ready. Parents want to feel they haven't lost a child, they've gained another son or daughter. Often they are so eager to keep family rituals and traditions the same ("We *always* spend New Year's Eve together") that they forget a newly married couple wants to launch their own traditions. Who gets "the kids" for the holidays often becomes a battleground.

285

If the families live near each other, it's sometimes judicious to split the day between his and her relatives. But when holidays involve long-distance travel, consider alternating holidays or even announcing, "We've decided to stay home for Christmas and spend it with friends. You are welcome to join *us.*"

WEDDING HORROR STORIES AND HAPPY ENDINGS

Even the best-laid wedding plans can be blown to smithereens.

Although most weddings go off without a hitch, here are a few horror stories to remind us that it's all in the attitude, and you'll survive if the baker tops the cake with the wrong flowers or red wine gets dribbled on the gown. (Remember, even Cinderella triumphed despite a lost slipper incident.) Besides, wedding disaster stories will keep your children entertained for years.

- A Texas bride and groom were lucky when the photographer arrived at their reception and immediately took a shot of the wedding cake, as was his custom. Just minutes later the cake tiers slipped apart and the cake completely collapsed. The photographer saved the day (or at least the keepsake album) by superimposing photographs of the predisaster cake with the couple cutting a slice from the collapsed cake.

- Consultant Robbi Ernst III recalls a Texas wedding where the bride's sister inadvertently dropped lipstick down the front of the wedding gown moments before the ceremony was to begin. "It went bouncing down her dress!" he recalls. The bride was in tears and the sister felt awful, until Ernst saved the day with his emergency supply kit. "I always have a clean cloth and club soda, so I dabbed at the stain and dried it with a hair dryer, then dusted the gown with talcum powder. It was hardly noticeable."

John Kozero is no stranger to wedding horror stories. He's heard whoppers. Like the bride whose little brother fingerpainted all over her gown the day before the wedding, or the pussycat who delivered a litter of kittens on top of a bride's beautiful white dress. But Kozero's stories all have happy endings, since the brides he hears about are all covered with wedding insurance they'd purchased from Fireman's Fund Insurance Co., of which Kozero is public relations director. Arranged by Association Program Managers and Fireman's Fund, Weddingsurance (see appendix) covers a wedding against unforeseeable events that could cause financial loss.

"Just about anything can block that trip down the aisle," Kozero says. It can be as personal as a serious illness or death in the family, as impersonal as an employer causing one of the couple to have to relocate across the country, or as gratuitous as a natural catastrophe like a windstorm, snowstorm, earthquake, or hurricane. Mother Nature throws tantrums and doesn't ask betrothed couples first.

"The primary purpose of this coverage," he says, "is to indemnify couples against losing a substantial amount of money if their wedding plans change. We want to help them protect that (average) $3,000 of nonrefundable deposits that could be forfeited if they change the date of the wedding."

Fireman's Fund offers two preset packages at $95 ("minimum") and $129 ("standard") premiums. The package features many provisions. For instance, if the photographer fails to appear or loses or damages the original negatives, the insurance covers up to $1,500 to retake the photos. During Operation Desert Storm, some couples were covered when their weddings were canceled due to military call-up.

A FINAL WORD FROM A BRIDE WITH THE RIGHT ATTITUDE

Oh, no! Snow!

When Laura DeMarkey and her fiancé planned a February wedding, her mother was worried. Both the bride and groom worked at a country club, so the February hiatus was the only time they could take a vacation. But February is also a common month for blizzards in their Connecticut town.

Not a flake of snow had fallen all winter long, but on the morning of the wedding, Laura and her mother awakened to the sound of snow plows. The ground was thickly covered in white.

"I said, 'Well, let's think positive,'" said Linda DeMarkey, Laura's mother. That upbeat attitude got them through the day. Although the bride had to cancel her makeup appointment, she managed to wade through the snow and get her hair done at a local salon. The florist called up to say she couldn't drive up the hill to the bride's home but would deliver the flowers to the church instead. And the limo driver managed to show up, despite closed roads and downed power lines.

"My husband had done a wonderful job shoveling the sidewalk, but I realized it was too narrow; Laura's gown was going to get wet. So I got the idea of getting an old sheet, cutting a hole in it, and spreading it out in the living room," said mom-to-the-rescue Linda DeMarkey.

She instructed her daughter to pull on snow boots and stand in the middle of the cut-out circle. Then relatives pulled up the four corners of the sheet and hoisted the wedding gown hem safely off the ground. They all tiptoed out to the limo, with the bride standing in the middle of the protective sheet.

Despite a power outage, failed traffic lights, and scenes of countless disabled cars along the way, the wedding party made it to the church. Some guests were stranded at home, but 67 of the 83 guests arrived. The wedding began as soon as everybody deposited their boots into a shopping bag at the church door.

"I was so proud. My daughter, the bride, was so positive! She said, 'This is going to be an adventure! This is going to be fun!' Not one complaint! And it turned out perfect."

289

Appendix

Bridal Publications and Newsletters

Magazines

Bride's and *Your New Home,* Conde Nast Publications, 350 Madison Ave., New York, NY 10017. (six issues yearly)

Bridal Guide, Globe Communications Corp., 441 Lexington Ave., New York, NY 10017. (six issues yearly)

Elegant Bride, Pace Communications, Inc., 1301 Carolina St., Greensboro, NC 27401. (six issues yearly)

Modern Bride, Cahners Publishing Company, 249 W. 17th St., New York, NY 10011. (six issues yearly)

You and Your Wedding, You and Your Wedding Publications, Ltd., 31-35 Beak St., London, England. (available in U.S. at major bookstore chains; six issues yearly)

Newspapers

Wedding Belles, 1601 Fulton Ave., Sacramento, CA 95825; (914) 481-6760. (six issues yearly)

Computer Software

The Wedding Workshop Software for Windows and Macintosh, Microprecision Software, Inc., Santa Clara, California. Includes a manual for brides and grooms.

Emily Post's Complete Guide to Weddings, by Elizabeth L. Post. HarperCollins Interactive, 1995. Includes a copy of *Emily Post's Complete Book of Wedding Etiquette.* (Windows CD-ROM)

Chapter 1: Announcing

For more information about gemstones:

> Gembureau
> The International Colored Gemstone Association
> 609 Fifth Ave., Suite 905
> New York, NY 10017

For a free consumer kit on diamonds and fine jewelry:

> American Gem Society
> 8881 W. Sahara Ave.
> Las Vegas, NV 89117

For a free copy of *Avoiding the Wedding Bell Blues:*

> New York City Department of Consumer Affairs
> 42 Broadway
> New York, NY 10004

For a list of member jewelers in your area and a free copy of the brochures *What You Should Know about Cultured Pearls* and *What You Should Know about Buying a Diamond:*

> Jewelers of America
> 1185 Avenue of the Americas, 30th Fl.
> New York, NY 10036
> 1-800-223-0673

For a free booklet, *Your Guide to Diamond Quality and Value,* and a brochure on engagement-ring spending guidelines:

Diamond Information Center
Worldwide Plaza
825 Eighth Ave., 36th Fl.
New York, NY 10019-7498

For information on platinum jewelry and the brochure, *What You Need to Know about Platinum:*

Platinum Guild International USA
620 Newport Center Dr., Suite 910
Newport Beach, CA 92660

If you suspect a jeweler has made a fraudulent claim about the stone you've purchased:

The Department of Consumer Affairs Complaint Division
42 Broadway
New York, NY 10004

The Jewelers' Vigilance Committee
401 East 34th St., Suite N 13A
New York, NY 10016

For information on wedding and engagement rings:

Lisa Lebowitz Cader, *The Perfect Ring: A Complete Guide to Buying the Ring of Your Dreams* (Kansas City, Mo.: Andrews and McMeel, a Universal Press Syndicate, 1993). $9.95, paperback.

Antoinette Matlin, Antonio Bonanno, and Jane Crystal, *Engagement and Wedding Rings: The Definitive Buying Guide for People in Love* (South Woodstock, Vt.: Gemstone Press, 1990). $14.95, paperback.

The Cultured Pearl Associations of America and Japan
Tele-Press Associates
321 E. 53rd St.
New York, NY 10022
(212) 688-5580

For information on engagements and etiquette:

Margorie Engel, *Weddings for Complicated Families: The New Etiquette for Couples with Divorced Parents and Those Planning a Remarriage* (Boston: Mount Ivey Press, 1993). $14.95, paperback.

Judith Martin, *Miss Manners on (Painfully Proper) Weddings* (New York: Crown Publishers, 1995). $14, hardcover.

Pamela A. Piljac, *The Bride's Thank-You Guide: Thank-You Writing Made Easy* (Chicago: Bryce Waterton Publications, 1988). $4.95, paperback.

Elizabeth L. Post, *Emily Post on Weddings* (New York: Harper Perennial, 1994). $6, paperback.

Elizabeth L. Post, *Emily Post's Complete Book of Wedding Etiquette* (New York: Harper Collins, 1991). $22, hardcover.

John Barry Ryan and Francis J. Lodato, *Creating Your Christian Engagement* (Ligouri, Mo.: Liguori Publications, 1994). $6.95, paperback.

Marjabelle Young Stewart, *Can My Bridesmaids Wear Black?: And 325 Other Most-Asked Etiquette Questions* (New York: St. Martin's Press, 1989). $8.95, paperback.

Martha A. Woodham, *The Bride Did What? Etiquette for the Wedding Impaired* (Atlanta: Longstreet Press, 1994). $14, hardcover; author is etiquette editor for *Elegant Bride* magazine.

To request a Presidential congratulatory note:

White House Greetings Office
1600 Pennsylvania Ave,. N.W.
Washington, D.C. 20500
(212) 688-5580

Chapter 2: Budget and Planning

If planning a wedding in a hurry, consult:

Bride's Magazine editors, with Kathy C. Mullins, *Bride's Shortcuts and Strategies for a Beautiful Wedding* (New York: Putnam Publishing Group, 1986). $7, paperback.

For general wedding planning information:

Janet Anastasio and Michelle Bevilacqua, *The Everything Wedding Book: Everything You Need to Know to Survive Your Wedding Day and Actually Even Enjoy It* (Holbrook, Mass.: Bob Adams, Inc., 1994). $12, paperback.

Bride's Magazine editors, *Bride's Book of Etiquette* (New York: Conde Nast Publications, 1993). $15.95, paperback.

Danielle Claro, *How to Have the Wedding You Want* (New York: Berkeley Books, 1995). $12, paperback.

Harriette Cole, fashion ed., *Essence* magazine, *Jumping the Broom: The African-American Wedding Planner* (New York: Henry Holt and Co., 1993). $27.50, hardcover.

Denise and Alan Fields, *Bridal Bargains: Secrets to Throwing a Fantastic Wedding on a Realistic Budget* 3rd edition (Boulder, Colo.: Windsor Peak Press, 1996). $11.95, paperback.

Edith Gilbert, *The Complete Wedding Planner* (New York: Warner Books, 1989). $11.99, paperback.

Winifred Gray, *You and Your Wedding* (New York: Bantam Books, 1985). $4.95, paperback.

Deanne Hudak and Darlene Hudak Rougeau, *The Bride's Organizer* (New York: Ballantine Books, 1993). $4.99, paperback.

Cele Goldsmith Lalli, *Modern Bride* editor-in-chief, *Modern Bride Guide to Etiquette* (New York: John Wiley & Sons, 1993). $12.95, paperback.

Cele Goldsmith Lalli, *Modern Bride* editor-in-chief, and Stephanie H. Dahl, *Modern Bride Wedding Celebrations: The Complete Wedding Planner for Today's Bride* (New York: John Wiley & Sons, 1992). $14.95, paperback.

295

Teddy Lenderman, *The Complete Idiot's Guide to the Perfect Wedding* (Indianapolis: Alpha Books, 1995). $16.99, paperback.

Ruth Muzzy and R. Kent Hughes, *The Christian Wedding Planner* (Wheaton, Ill.: Tyndale House Publishers, 1991). $15, paperback.

Pamela A. Piljac, *The Bride-to-Be Book: A Complete Wedding Planner for the Bride* (Portage, Ind.: Bryce-Waterton Publications, 1989). $9.95, paperback.

Mimi Pond, *A Groom of One's Own, and Other Bridal Accessories* (New York: Penguin Books, 1991). $14.95, hardcover.

Jacqueline Smith, *The Creative Wedding Idea Book: Bold Suggestions to Make Every Aspect of Your Wedding Special* (Holbrook, Mass.: Bob Adams, Inc., 1994). $12, paperback.

Marjabelle Young Stewart, *Your Complete Wedding Planner* (New York: St. Martin's Press, 1989). $14.95, paperback.

Martha Stewart, with text by Elizabeth Hawes, *Martha Stewart's Weddings* (New York: Clarkson N. Potter, 1987). $70 hardcover.

Martha Stewart, *The Wedding Planner* (New York: Clarkson N. Potter, 1988). $35; spiral-bound hardcover with pockets.

Carroll Stoner, *Weddings for Grown-ups: Everything You Need to Know to Plan Your Wedding Your Way* (San Francisco: Chronicle Books, 1983). $12.95, paperback.

Pamela Thomas, *Bridal Guide: A Complete Guide on How to Plan Your Wedding* (La Crosse, Wis.: Fifth Avenue Brides Publishing Co., 1989). $12.95, paperback.

Planning a Wedding to Remember (Carpenteria, Calif.: Wilshire Publications, 1992). $15.95, paperback.

For planning books geared to the groom:

Paula Begoun and Stephanie Bell, *There Must Be Something for the Groom to Do* (Emeryville, Calif.: Publishers Group West, 1996). $12.95, paperback.

Peter N. Nelson, *Marry Like a Man: The Essential Guide for Grooms* (New York: Penguin Books USA, 1992). $10, paperback.

Thomas M. Piljac, *The Groom to Groom Book: A Complete Wedding Planner for the Groom* (Chicago: Bryce-Waterton Publications, an imprint of Chicago Review Press, 1990). $9.95, paperback.

Nancy Robison, *Dear Son, About Your Wedding: A Guide for the Groom* (New York: Fireside Books, 1989). $5.95, paperback.

Chapter 3: Wedding Consultants

For information on wedding consultants or for a referral to a consultant in your area:

The Association of Bridal Consultants (A.B.C.)
200 Chestnutland Rd.
New Milford, CT 96776-2521
(203) 355-0564
(A.B.C. also offers a free brochure, *Do You Need a Bridal Consultant?*)

June Wedding, Inc.,® An Association for Event Professionals
8514 FM 3117
Temple, TX 76501-7206
(817) 983-3596
Email: junewed@vvm.com;
URL: http://www.dpatch.com/JWI
(June Wedding, Inc.,® also provides referrals to special-event professionals for corporate and private parties)

National Bridal Service (N.B.S.)
3122 West Cary St.
Richmond, VA 23221
(804) 355-0464

The Association of Certified Professional Wedding Consultants
7791 Prestwick Circle
San Jose, CA 95135
(408) 223-5686

For information on the role of the wedding consultant:

Teddy Lenderman, *The Complete Idiot's Guide to the Perfect Wedding* (Indianapolis: Alpha Books, 1995). $16.99, paperback. See particularly the "Wake Me When It's Over" chapter.

Chapter 4: The Bridal Registry

L.L. Bean
Gift Registry Service
Freeport, ME
1-800-341-4341, ext. 3226

Macy's
Bridal Registry
1-800-459-2743

Bullock's Bridal Registry
1-800-622-9748

The Home Depot
Bridal Registry Service
Atlanta, GA
(404) 433-8211

Crate and Barrel
Bridal Registry
1-800-967-6696

Marshall Field's
Bridal Registry
1-800-243-6436

Club WEDD
Target Stores
Minneapolis, MN
1-800-888-WEDD

JCPenney
The Gift Registry
1-800-JCP-GIFT

Filene's
1-800-4-BRIDES

JCPenney Gift Registry Catalog
P.O. Box 2021
Milwaukee, WI 53201-2021
1-800-527-4438

Service Merchandise
Bridal Registry
1-800-251-1212

Williams Sonoma
1-800-541-2233

For information on registering silver, china, and housewares, contact these companies for referrals to bridal registries in your area:

Lenox
1-800-63-LENOX

Royal Doulton
1-800-68-CHINA

Pfaltzgraf
1-800-499-1976

KitchenAid
1-800-541-6390

Reed & Barton
1-800-343-1383

Mikasa
1-800-833-4681

Noritake
1-800-562-1991

Fortunoff
1-800-814-9311

Denby Pottery
1-800-551-9050

Gorham
P.O. Box 906
Mount Kisco, NY 10549

Farberware
(212) 683-9660

Waterford Crystal
1-800-523-0009

Oneida Silversmith
1-800-877-6667

Krups
1-800-526-5377

Wedgwood
1-800-622-8345

Chapter 5: Parties and Showers

Janet Anastazio, *The Wedding Shower Book* (Holbrook, Mass.: Bob Adams Inc., 1995). $6.95, paperback.

Jo Chapman, *Wedding Parties and Showers: Planning Memorable Celebrations* (New York: Sterling Publishing Co., 1993). $5.95, paperback.

Beverly Clark, *Showers* (Carpenteria, Calif.: Wilshire Publications, 1989). $8.95, paperback.

Sharon E. Dlugosch and Florence E. Nelson, *Bridal Showers: 50 Great Ideas for a Perfect Shower* (New York: Perigee Books, 1984). $9, paperback.

Gail Greco, *Bridal Shower Handbook: The Complete Guide to Planning the Perfect Wedding* (Radnor, Pa.: Wallace Homestead Books, 1988). $11.95, paperback.

Ann Landers, *The Ann Landers Guide for Brides* (1987; distributed as a reader service by your local newspaper and Creators Syndicate, Inc., P.O. Box 11562, Chicago, IL 60611-0562). $3.75, paperback.

Bruce Moulton, *Bridal Shower Journal* (Wayzata, Minn.: Lakeland Color Press, 1995). $16.95, printed on acid-free paper, the keepsake journal includes pocket pages to hold cards, lists, and mementos, plus enclosed thank-you notes and envelopes.

Chapter 6: Dressing the Bride and Wedding Party

Larry Goldman, *Dressing the Bride* (New York: Crown Publishers, 1993). $40, hardcover; a beautiful coffee-table book featuring sumptuous color photographs, glossaries, and facts about every fabric, trim, and style imaginable; a great source for coordinating a total wedding ensemble, written and photographed by a leading fashion photographer.

Jo Packham, *Wedding Gowns and Other Bridal Apparel* (New York: Sterling Publishing Co., 1994). $5.95, paperback.

For a free copy of "Your Formalwear Guide," to advise men for day and evening weddings, send a stamped, self-addressed envelope to:

The International Formalwear Association
401 North Michigan Ave.
Chicago, IL 60611

For information about gown restoration, get help from your local historical society, costume institute, or textile museum, or contact:

Sewtique
391 Long Hill Rd.
Groton, CT 06340
(203) 445-7320
1-800-332-9122 (CT only)
Textile specialist Evelyn Kennedy refurbishes gowns mailed in from all over the world. She has restored a Civil War–era gown, Najavo rugs, as well as vintage samplers and tapestries.

For information on gown preservation, cleaning and archival-quality preservation products:

National Gown Cleaners
4100 Moorpark Ave.
San Jose, CA 95117
(408) 241-3490
(415) 962-1997

For information on sewing your own wedding attire and veils for the bride, mothers, and attendants:

Naomi Baker and Tammy Young, *Craft an Elegant Wedding* (Radnor, Pa.: Chilton Book Co., 1995). $17.95, paperback.

Chapter 7: Wedding Cakes

Rose Levy Beranbaum, *The Cake Bible* (New York: William Morrow and Co., 1988). $27.50, hardcover. This book includes recipes and color photographs of wedding cakes created by the caterer and cookbook author for major women's magazines. Also included, a comprehensive "Foolproof Formulas and Techniques for Making Large and Special Occasion Cakes" chapter. With tips for storing and transporting the finished products.

Flo Braker, *The Simple Art of Perfect Baking* (Shelbourne, Vt.: Chapters Publishing, 1992). $19.95, paperback. A complete baking guide for novice through impassioned professional.

Alice Medrich, *Cocolat: Extraordinary Chocolate Desserts* (New York: Warner Books, 1990). $35, hardcover. Sumptuous photographs, great recipes, and ideas for decorating.

Colette Peters, *Colette's Wedding Cakes* (Boston: Little, Brown and Co., 1995). $35, hardcover. Includes more than 32 recipes and detailed instructions for traditional and unusual wedding cakes, from a classic Victorian design to cakes shaped as bells, hearts, and hats.

Colette Peters, *Colette's Cakes: The Art of Cake Decorating* (Boston: Little, Brown And Co., 1991). $35, hardcover. Includes step-by-step directions, photos, and line drawings for creating wedding and special-occasion cakes.

Martha Stewart, *Entertaining* (New York: Clarkson N. Potter, 1982). $35, hardcover. See especially "The At-Home Wedding" chapter and recipe for a tiered wedding cake.

Chapter 8: Wedding Flowers

Nancy Kahan, with Eleanor Berman, *Entertaining for Business: A Complete Guide to Creating Special Events with Style and a Personal Touch* (New York: Clarkson N. Potter, 1990). $40, hardcover. Great inspiration, with stunning photographs of centerpieces created by premier party planners and floral designers.

Shirley Monckton, *The Complete Book of Wedding Flowers* (London: Casell Books, 1993). $19.95, hardcover.

Jo Packham, *Wedding Flowers: Choosing and Making Beautiful Bouquets and Arrangements* (New York: Sterling Publishing Co., 1993). $5.95, paperback.

Tom Pritchard and Billy Jarecki, *Madderlake's Trade Secrets: Straight Talk about Finding and Arranging Flowers Naturally* (New York: Clarkson N. Potter, 1992). $40.00, hardcover. Tips from the famous New York flower shop that has designed flowers for White House state dinners, weddings, and other gatherings.

Chapter 9: Photography and Videography

For referrals to photographers in your area:

Professional Photographers of America Association
57 Forsyth St., Suite 1600
Atlanta, GA 30303
(404) 522-8600

Chapter 10: Invitations and Favors

(See also etiquette books listed in this appendix for chapter 2)

Naomi Baker and Tammy Young, *Craft an Elegant Wedding* (Radnor, Pa.: Chilton Books, 1995). $17.95, paperback. Includes directions for handcrafted favors and accessories.

Bride's Magazine editors, *Bride's All-New Book of Etiquette* (New York: Putnam Publishing Group, 1993). $15.95, paperback.

Cele Goldsmith Lalli, editor-in-chief, *Modern Bride* magazine, *Modern Bride Guide to Etiquette* (New York: John Wiley & Sons, 1993). $12.95, paperback.

Elizabeth L. Post, *Emily Post's Wedding Planner* (New York: Harper Collins, 1991). $7.50, paperback.

Diane Warner, *Beautiful Wedding Decorations and Gifts on a Small Budget* (Cincinnati: Betterways Books, 1995). $12.99, paperback. Includes ideas for wedding favors.

For decorative photo stamps of the bride and groom, (*not* for use as U.S. postage stamps):

Photo Stamp, Inc.
55 West Red Oak Lane
Mail Drop MB-95
White Plains, NY 10604
1-800-644-STAMPS

For live tree seedlings and seed packets:

The Greenworld Project
84 Broadway
Kingston, NY 12401

Celebrations in Green
By Expressions
P.O. Box 92-MB4
Manchester, PA 17345
(717) 266-6519

Chapter 12: The Wedding Ceremony

Wedding Vows and Rituals:

Don Altman, *151 Ways to Make Your Wedding Special* (Los Angeles: Moon Lake Media, 1994). $9.95, paperback.

Janet Anastasio and Michelle Bevilacqua, *The Everything Wedding Vows Book* (Holbrook, Mass.: Bob Adams Inc., 1994). $6, paperback.

Joseph M. Champlin, *Together for Life* (Notre Dame, Ind.: Ave Maria Press,). This booklet for Catholics is available from your parish priest.

Harriet Cole, *Jumping the Broom Wedding Workbook* (New York: Henry Holt and Co., 1996). $16.95, paperback.

Anita Diamont, *The New Jewish Wedding* (New York: Simon & Schuster, 1985). $10, paperback.

Barbara Eklof, *With These Words . . . I Thee Wed: Contemporary Wedding Vows for Today's Couples* (Holbrook, Mass.: Bob Adams, Inc., 1989). $7.95, paperback.

Roger Fritts, *For as Long as We Both Shall Live* (New York: Avon Books, 1993). $10, paperback.

Winifred Gray, *You and Your Wedding* (New York: Bantam Books, 1985). $4.95, paperback. Great source for information on religious ceremonies.

Peg Kehret, *Wedding Vows* (Colorado Springs, Colo.: Meriwether Publications, 1989). $12, paperback.

Cele Goldsmith Lalli and Stephanie H. Dahl, *Modern Bride Wedding Celebrations* (New York: John Wiley & Sons, Inc., 1992). $14.95, paperback. Information on interfaith marriage.

Sydney Barbara Metrick, *I Do: A Guide to Creating Your Own Unique Ceremony* (Berkeley, Calif.: Celestial Arts Publishing, 1992). $11.95, paperback.

Eleanor Munro, ed., *Wedding Readings: Centuries of Writing and Rituals for Love and Marriage* (New York: Viking Press, 1989). $22.50, hardcover.

Arlene Hamilton Stewart, *The Bride's Book of Wedding Traditions* (New York: Hearst Books, 1995). $18, hardcover. Wedding ceremonies, customs, and superstitions.

For information on the Family Medallion, and Vessel and the Rose ceremonies:

Clergy Services, Inc.
706 West 42nd St.
Kansas City, MO 64111
(816) 753-3886
1-800-237-1922

Chapter 13: Music

Books, Compact Discs, Cassettes, and Video

Len Handler, compiler, *The Perfect Wedding Song Book* (Port Chester, N.Y.: Cherry Lane Music Co., 1991). $16.95, paperback. Includes sheet music for every portion of the ceremony, with tips on hiring musicians.

Pamela Thomas, *Bridal Guide: A Complete Guide on How to Plan Your Wedding* (La Crosse, Wis.: Bridal Guide Ltd., 1989). $12.95, paperback. Lists more than 400 music selections by title, composer, and publisher.

For a list of band leaders in your area:

The Orchestra Leaders Association
348 Willis Ave.
Mineola, NY 11501
1-800-359-0859

For sheet music, a compact disc, or cassette tape of original contemporary music for weddings:

New Traditions
P.O. Box 827
East Longmeadow, MA 01028
1-800-44-SONGS

For the *Here Comes the Bride* music video showcasing wedding music and examples of different instrument ensembles in 40 different weddings:

MBC Video, Inc.
14415 NE 64th St.
Redmond, WA 98052
(206) 885-7934
Enclose check or money order for $24.95, plus $5 shipping and handling.

305

Chapter 14: Reception and Catering

(See also bridal planning guides listed in chapter 1)

For money-saving tips:

Sharon Naylor, *1001 Ways to Save Money and Still Have a Dazzling Wedding* (Chicago: Contemporary Books, 1994). $9.95, paperback.

Diane Warner, *How to Have a Big Wedding on a Small Budget* (Cincinnati: Writer's Digest Books, 1992). $12.99, paperback.

For a listing of 2,000 reception sites in 10 cities nationwide:

Hannelore Hahn and Tatiana Stoumen, *Places: A Directory of Public Places for Private Events and Private Places for Public Functions*, 7th ed. (New York: Tenth House Enterprises, Inc., 1991). $24.95, paperback.

For more information on wedding levels of formality:

Winifred Gray, *You and Your Wedding* (New York: Bantam Books, 1985). $4.95, paperback.

For a complete guide to planning a reception, including catering tips and checklists:

Jo Packham, *Wedding Receptions: Arranging a Joyous Celebration* (New York: Sterling Publishing Co., 1993). $5.95, paperback.

Chapter 16: Honeymoon Travel

For free brochures *Why to Use an ASTA Travel Agent, Travel Safely,* and *Avoiding Travel Problems:*

The American Society of Travel Agents
World Headquarters
1101 King St.
Alexandria, VA 22314
(703) 739-2783

For free, 24-page *Cruising* booklet:

Cruise Lines International Association
500 Fifth Ave., Suite 1407
New York, NY 10110

For information on limousines:

National Limousine Association
1300 L. Street NW, Suite 1050
Washington, DC 20005
1-800-NLA-7007

For Help Planning a Destination Wedding

Creative Leisure International
951 Transport Way
Petaluma, CA 94975
1-800-426-6367
Specializes in destination weddings in Hawaii and U.S. Virgin Islands.

Antiqua and Barbuda Tourist Office
610 Fifth Ave., Suite 311
New York, NY 10020
(212) 541-4117
For information about civil or religious wedding ceremonies in this twin-island Caribbean nation requiring no waiting time for marriage license.

Weddings and Honeymoons at Walt Disney World Resort in Florida
(407) 828-3400 For information on Disney's Fairy Tale Weddings
(407) 827-7200 For information on honeymoons at Disneyworld resorts

International Ventures
65 Old Ridgefield Rd.
Wilton, CT 06987
Specializes in destination weddings and luxury safaris in Africa and the Seychelles Islands.

Geri Bain, travel editor *Modern Bride* magazine, *Modern Bride Honeymoons and Weddings Away* (New York: John Wiley and Sons, 1995). $14.95, paperback.

307

Denise and Alan Fields, *Far and Away Weddngs: Secrets to Planning a Long Distance Wedding* (Boulder, Colo.: Windsor Peak Press, 1994). $8.95, paperback.

Exotic-Travel Services

Adventures
P.O. Box 1336
Bozeman, MT 59771
1-800-231-7422
Specializes in travel to Costa Rica, Belize, Honduras, Baja and Montana.

Journeys International
4011 Jackson Rd.
Ann Arbor, MI 48103
1-800-255-8735
Specializes in exotic destinations in 30 countries in Asia, Latin America, East Africa, Costa Rica, and Tibet.

Lost World Adventures
1189 Autumn Ridge Dr.
Marietta, GA 30066
1-800-999-0558
Specializes in exotic trips to the Amazon rain forest, including bird-watching, mountain biking, and river-rafting expeditions.

Chapter 17: Stress, Happy Endings, and Preparation for Marriage

Stephanie H. Dahl, *Modern Bride Just Married: Everything You Need to Know to Plan Your Life Together* (New York: John Wiley & Sons, 1994). $12.95, paperback.

Jerry D. Hardin, M.S. and Diane C. Sloan, M.S., *Getting Ready for Marriage Workbook: How to Really Get to Know the Person You're Going to Marry* (Nashville: Thomas Nelson Publishers, 1992). $14.99, paperback.

Abigail Kirsch with Susan M. Greenberg, *The Bride and Groom's First Cookbook* (New York: Doubleday, 1996). $25, hardcover.

Ellen Sue Stern, *I Do: Meditations for Brides* (New York: Dell Publishing Co., 1993). $8.99, paperback. Wise and witty words of encouragement for newly-weds for every day of the first year of marriage.

Michelle Burhard Thomas, *An Introduction to Marriage and Family Therapy* (New York: Merrill, 1992). $40.25, hardcover.

Peggy Vaughan and James Vaughn, Ph.D., *Making Love Stay: Everything You Ever Knew about Love But Forgot* (Los Angeles: Lowell House, 1992). $22.95, hardcover.

American Association of Marriage and Family Therapists (A.A.M.F.T.)
1100 17th St. NW
Washington, DC 20036-4601
(202) 467-5105

PAIRS Foundation, Ltd.
3705 S. George Mason Dr., Suite C8s
Falls Church, VA 22041
(703)988-5550
1-800-477-2477

Wedding Insurance:

Fireman's Fund *Weddingsurance*
Association of Program Managers
777 San Marin Dr.
Novato, CA 94945-9975
1-800-ENGAGED

Index

A-line bridal silhouette, 91, 93
Accessories
    attire and jewelry, 104-106
    decorative and floral, 138-139, 144
    party favors, 177-188
Age difference, 280-281
Alençon lace, 99
American Society of Travel Agents
    (ASTA), 261, 263-264, 268
Announcements
    announcing marriage to children, 4
    engagement, 1-23
    newspaper, 8-12
    wedding, 164
    wording, 8-13
    worksheet, engagement, 12-13
    worksheet, wedding, 10-11
Association of Bridal Consultants
    (A.B.C.), 56, 59, 229
Association of Certified Professional
    Wedding Consultants, 59

Attire (see also Gown)
    accessories and jewelry, 104-106
    average cost of gown, 88-89
    bridal gown, 87-101
    bridesmaids, 107-109
    child attendants, 110-111
    (for) civil ceremony, 192
    fabrics, 100-101
    figure flattery, 93-94
    headpiece and veil, 89, 102-104
    laces, 98-99
    men's formalwear, 111-114
    mother of bride/mother of groom,
        32, 110
    preservation and cleaning, 114-117
    shoes, 89
    shop, where to, 94-95
    silhouettes, 90-94
    sleeves, 97-98
    symbolic meaning of gown, 202
    train, 101
    ushers, 114

～ B ～

Bachelor party, 84-85
Ball gown bridal silhouette, 91
Ballet length veil, 103
Balloon sleeves, 97
Banns, 189, 261
Barillo, John, 211
Basque waist, 92
Batiste fabric, 100
Battenberg lace, 99
Best man, 52-53
Blusher veil, 103
Blouson bridal silhouette, 91
Bouquet, 136-138 (see also Flowers)
    arm bouquet, 137
    Biedermeier, 137
    breakaway (tossing), 137
    bridesmaid's, 137
    cascade, 137
    hand-tied, 137
    nosegay, 137
    pomander, 137
    spray, 137
    symbolic meaning of, 205
Box storage, 116
Bratten, Millie Martini, 188
Bride's magazine, 188
Bridesmaid(s)
    choosing, 21
    declining invitation to be, 20
    dresses, 107-109,
    number of, 20, 228-229
    party honoring, 83-84
    roles of, 53
    symbolic meaning of, 202
    traditional expenses of, 43
Brocade, 100

Broken engagement, 7
Bruneau, Patricia, 27-28, 62, 180
Brussels lace, 99
Budget (and planning), 23-54
    compromise, 26-27
    expectations, 24-29
    traditional responsibilities
        bride and her family, 41-42
        bride and groom, 43
        bridesmaid(s), 43
        groom and his family, 42
        ushers, 43
    vendor costs, average, 51
    wedding worksheet, 44-50
Buffet, 243, 246
Bustle, 101-102

～ C ～

Cake, wedding, 21, 119-130
    bridesmaids' cake, 83-84
    costs, 122-123
    cutting ceremony, 125
    cutting fee, 248
    decorations, 127-129
    glazes and frostings, 126-127
    groom's cake, 124
    history of, 120
    serving yields, 129
    symbolic meaning of, 119,125
Calendar, planning, 30-39
Calligraphy, 164
Candlelight ceremony, 194
Cap sleeve, 97
Carat weight, 13-14
Card, 159-178 (see also Invitations)
    ceremony, 165

informals, 166
pew, 165
reception, 165
response, 165
Carter, Michael, 152
Catering, 241-253
    budget, percentage of, 51
    buffet, 243, 246
    choosing caterer, 242
    cost-cutting tips, 251-253
    dance floor, 244-245
    food stations, 243, 247
    questions to ask caterer,
        249-251
    styles of table service,
        245-247
    table sizes, 244
    terms, 248-249
Casolino, Sandra, 29
Ceremony, wedding, 185-212
    (see also Theme weddings)
    candlelight, 194
    Catholic, 186, 189, 200
    civil, 192
    double wedding, 193
    family medallion, 195
    gay, 283-284
    interfaith, 187-188
    Jewish, 189-191, 201, 236
    military, 193
    Mormon, 192
    music for, 218-220
    Protestant, 191-192
    questions to ask officiant,
        199-201
    unity candle, 194
    vessel and the rose, 195
    vows, 197-198

Chantilly lace, 99
Chapel veil, 103
Chiffon, 100
Children, 179-184
    attendants, 110-111, 181
        flower girl, 181
        junior bridesmaid, 181
        ring bearer, 181
    attire, 110-111, 183
    including in ceremony/reception,
        182-183, 195-196
    notifying of wedding plans, 4
    objections to remarriage, 280-282
    photographing, 154, 183-184
Chuppah, 189
Clarity of diamond, 13-14
Coleman, Rev. Roger, 195,197
Color of diamond, 13-14
Consultants, wedding, 26-28, 55-66
    Association of Bridal Consultants
        (A.B.C.), 56, 59, 229
    Association of Certified
        Professional Wedding
        Consultants, 59
    Bruneau, Patricia, 27-28, 62, 180
    Dembo, Beverly, 57
    Ernst, Robbi, III, 27, 51, 60, 62,
        232-233, 286-287
    fees, 58
    Foresta, Benita, 89, 91, 93
    Greenamyer, Gaye, 58, 61
    Hodges, Michelle, 63
    June Wedding, Inc.®, 51, 59
    Lenderman, Teddy, 58
    Monaghan, Gerard, 56
    National Bridal Service (N.B.S.), 59
    questions to ask, 63-65
    Rosenfield, Lyn, 58, 61

roles of, 61-65
Sorenson, Annena, 199, 271
Winkelstein, Denise, 26, 62, 207
Contracts
    flowers, 135
    photography, 152-153
Creative Leisure International,
    259
Credit card, 96, 263, 266, 278
Crinoline, 100
Cruise, 265, 267
Customs, 201-212
    bridesmaids, 202
    bouquet, 205
    dowry, 2-3, 186, 207
    ethnic, 206-210
    family customs and traditions,
      274,285
    gown, 204-205
    honeymoon, 203
    kiss, wedding, 203
    ring, 204
    something old, something new,
      206
    trousseau, 202
    ushers, 203
    veil, 202
Cut of diamond, 13-14
Cutaway tuxedo, 114

D

Dance floor, 244-245
DeMarkey, Laura, 288-289
DeMarkey, Linda, 288-289
Dembo, Beverly, 57
Department of Consumer Affairs, 18

Destination Wedding, 235-236, 256,
    258-261(see also Honeymoons)
    marrying abroad, 31, 260-261
Diamond (see also Ring)
    carat weight, 13-14
    clarity, 13-14
    color, 13-14
    cut, 13-14
    four Cs, 13-17
    myths, 19
    shapes, 13-14
Disc jockey, 217
Disneyworld (Disney weddings), 258
Dowry, 2-3, 186, 207
Dressing (see also Attire)
    mother of the bride, 32
    mother of the groom, 32

E

Elopement, 284-285
Empire bridal silhouette, 91, 93
Engagement, 1-23
    announcement, wording, 9-13
    average length, 6-7
    broken, 7
    gifts, 4-6
    party, 4-6
    photographs, 8
    ring, 6, 7, 13-17,105
Engraving, 163, 230-231,
Ernst, Robbi, III, 27, 51, 60, 62,
    232-233, 286-287
Ethnic customs and traditions
    African-American, 206-207
    Chinese, 210
    English, 210

German, 209
Greek, 209-210
Hispanic, 207
Irish, 209
Italian, 208
Japanese, 208
Jewish, 207, 236
Polish, 210
Scottish, 210
Etiquette
honeymoon planning, 256
who pays, 25
wording of invitations
Expectations, 24-29
worksheet, 28-29

~ F ~

Fabrics, wedding gown, 100-101, 117
batiste, 100
brocade, 100
chiffon, 100
chintz, 100
crinoline, 100
faille, 100
illusion, 100
jersey, 100
linen, 100
moire, 100
organdy, 100
organza, 100
satin, 101
shantung, 100
silk, 101,
taffeta, 100
voile, 100
Favors, party, 177-178

Fireman's Fund Insurance, 287-288
Flowers, 129-142
alternatives to, 137, 142
artificial, 135-136
bouquet, 136-138
boutonniere, 138
checklist, 143-144
choosing a florist, 132-134
contract, 135
cost, 132, 138-141
edible, for wedding cake, 128
floral headpiece, 137
symbolic meaning of, 130, 205
traditional meanings of, 141-142
Flower girl, 181, 230
Food stations, 243
Foresta, Benita, 89, 91
Formality, levels of
formal wedding , 231
informal wedding , 231
semiformal wedding , 231
ultraformal wedding, 230
Formalwear, men's, 111-114
Four Cs, 13-14
Freitag, Steve, 237

~ G ~

Gauntlet sleeve, 97
Gay marriage, 283-284
Geiger, Gregory, 149, 212
Gembureau, 16-17
Gemstone, 15-18
Gifts (see also Registry)
(for) attendants, 37
engagement, 5
of money, 11, 21, 206

returning, 7
shower, 81-84
wedding obligation, 22, 164
Gloves, 105
Goldman, Larry, 98
Goodie bag, 40-41
Gown, wedding (see also Attire)
    costs, 88-89
    preservation and cleaning of,
        114-117
    protecting in inclement weather,
        289
    symbolic meaning of, 204-205
Greenamyer, Gaye, 58, 61
Greenberg, Earle, 146
Greenberg, Joel, 146
Greenworld Project, 178
Guest list, 161-162

⌐ ℋ ⌐

Headpiece
    average costs, 89
    floral, 137-143
    styles
        backpiece, 103
        garden hat, 103
        headband, 102
        juliet cap, 103
        mantilla, 103
        picture hat, 103
        pillbox, 102
        profile, 103
        tiara, 103
        wreath, 102
Herbs, 142, 205
Hodgins, Laura Torres, 106-107

Holiday wedding
    boutonniere, 138
    favors, 178
    theme, 233-244
Honeymoon, 255-268
    all-inclusive package, 264-265
    average costs, 261-262
    average length, 259
    cruise, 265, 267
    destination wedding honeymoon,
        235, 256, 259-261
    destinations, 257
    packing for, 265-266
    time-share resort, 264
Horror stories, wedding, 286-289

⌐ ℐ ⌐

Illusion fabric, 100
In-laws
    holidays with, 285-286
    problems with, 278-279
Insurance
    reception site, 238
    rings, 15
    wedding, 287-288
Interfaith wedding
    ceremony, 187-188
    stress, 271
International Formalwear
    Association, 112
International Ventures, 259-260
Invitations, 159-178
    calligraphy, 164
    ceremony card, 165
    costs, 51, 60
    engraving, 230-231

(for) formal wedding, 231
guest list, 161-162
handwritten, 164
home computer, 164
informal cards, 166
(for) informal wedding, 231
noting where registered, on
    shower invitation, 70
offset/laser printing, 164
pew card, 165
reception card, 165
response card, 165
(for) semiformal wedding, 231
thermography, 163-164
wedding announcement, 166
who issues, 160
when to order, 160
wording, 166-176
    bride's parents host, 168
    both sets of parents co-host,
        171
    contemporary, 175
    couple hosts, 170
    divorced parents host,
        170-171
    double wedding, 173
    etiquette, 166-167
    groom's family hosts, 172
    military titles, 167, 174-175
    private ceremony, 172
    parent(s) deceased, 168-170
    remarriage, 172

⌐ 𝒥 ⌐

James, Diane, 135-136
Jersey fabric, 100

Jewel neckline, 96
Jewelers of America, 13
Jewelers' Vigilance Committee, 18, 19
Jewelry, 104-105
Juliet cap, 103
Juliet sleeve, 97
Jumping the broom, 206
June Wedding, Inc.®, 27, 51, 59
Junior bridesmaid, 181

⌐ 𝒦 ⌐

Ketubah, 190
Keyhole neckline, 97
Kiss, symbolic meaning, 203
Kozero, John, 287
Kremkow, Cheryl, 15-16

⌐ 𝓛 ⌐

Lace, 98-99
    Alençon, 99
    Battenberg, 99
    Brussels, 99
    Chantilly, 99
    Point d'Esprit, 99
    Schiffli, 99
    Venise (Venice), 99
Lalli, Cele Goldsmith, 6
LaMarre, Jodie, 195
Landers, Ann, 162
Lefkowitz, Sandra, 236
Leg-o-mutton sleeve, 94, 98
Lenderman, Teddy, 58
License, marriage, 190
Lighting, 133

Linen, 100
Lowe, Tref, 156, 211
Lucas, Karen, 241

⌐ *M* ⌐

Makeup, 106, 107
Maid/matron of honor, 43, 52
Marrying abroad, 31, 260-261
Mayeux, Randy, 197-198
Military
    titles, 167
    wedding, 193
Miniskirt, 92
Modern Bride magazine, 167, 270
Moiré, 100
Monaghan, Gerard, 56
Months, popular for weddings,
    229
Morgan, Susan, 121, 129
Morrissey, Christine, 115-117
Mothers of bride/groom, 32, 110
Mushinsky, Elizabeth, 104, 176
Music, 213-225
    band size, 216
    ceremony, 218-220
    demo tapes, 214-215
    disc jockey, 217
    fees, 51, 214
    performers, types of, 222-223
    prelude, 218
    processional, 218
    recessional, 219
    reception, 221-222
    selections, 220-222
    questions to ask musicians,
        223-224

Myths
    marriage, 273-274
    wedding, 19-20

⌐ *N* ⌐

Name change, 277-278
National Bridal Service, 59
National Gown Cleaners, 115
Necklines, 96-97
    boat, 96
    fichu, 96
    illusionary, 97
    jewel, 96
    keyhole, 97
    off-the-shoulder, 97
    portrait, 96
    Queen Anne, 97
    Queen Elizabeth, 97
    square, 97
    sweetheart, 96
    V-neck, 97

⌐ *O* ⌐

Off-the-shoulder neckline, 97
Officiant
    fee, 51
    questions to ask, 199-201
Orchestra Leaders Association, 217
Organdy, 100
Organza, 100

~ *P* ~

Packing, tips for, 265-266
Papal blessing, 162
Parties, 77-86
    bachelor, 84-85
    bridal shower, 78-82
    engagement, 4-6
    rehearsal dinner, 86
Peters, Colette, 120
Photography, 145-155 (see also
    Videography)
    album trends, 150-151
    black and white, 151
    bridal portrait, 34-35
    children, 154, 183-184
    classic portraiture, 147-149
    engagement photos, 8
    equipment, 152
    finding a photographer, 149-150
    natural light, 149
    photojournalism, 148-149
    questions to ask photographer,
        154-155
    soft-focus, 149
Place cards
    chocolate, 129
    reception seating, 240-241
Planning, wedding, 23-54
Point d'Esprit lace, 99
Portrait
    neckline, 96
    bridal portrait, 34-35
Practical Application of Intimate
    Relationship Skills Foundation
    (PAIRS), 276
Pre-Cana preparation, 186-187,
    275-276

Pregnant
    attendant, 109
    bride, 279-280
Prenuptial agreement, 35, 284
Prepare and Enrich, 276
Preparation for marriage, 273-277
    doubts, 276-277
    PAIRS, 276
    Pre-Cana, 186-187, 275-276
    Prepare and Enrich, 276
    stress, 272
Preservation of gown, 114-117
President, announcement sent to, 162
Princess bridal silhouette, 92
Problems, travel, 268
Professional Photographers of
    America, 149-150
Program, wedding, 211
Proposal, wedding, 1-3

~ *Q* ~

Queen Anne neckline, 97
Queen Elizabeth neckline, 97
Queen Victoria, 204

~ *R* ~

Receiving line, 21
Reception, 227-253
    catering, 51, 241,253
    cost-cutting tips, 249-251
    levels of formality, 230-231
    music, 221-222
    questions to ask site manager,
        238-240

seating, 240-241
sites, 228-229,236-237
theme, 232-236
    black and white, 233
    destination, 235-236
    Halloween, 233
    holiday, 233-234
    nautical, 233
    progressive, 235
    Renaissance, 233
    snowball, 233
    Valentine, 234
    Victorian, 235
    weekend, 235
Regan, Susan, 19
Registry, bridal, 67-76
Rehearsal dinner, 86
Remarriage, 4, 21, 172
    children and, 4, 181-182,
        195-196, 280-282
    family medallion ceremony,
        195-196
Responsibilities
    best man, 52-53
    bridesmaid, 53
    maid/matron of honor, 52
    responsibility cards, 54
    usher, 53-54
    who does what, 52
    who pays for what, 41
Rienzo, Marie, 270
Ring, diamond
    amount to spend, 14-15
    carat, 13-14
    cut, 13-14
    Claddagh, 209
    clarity, 13-14
    color, 13-14

    during ceremony, 105,190
    engagement, 6, 7, 13-17
    fit, proper, 15
    four Cs, 13-14
    gemstones, 15-18
    selecting, 17-18
    symbolic meaning of, 204
Ringbearer, 181, 230
Roman, Michael, 13
Rosenfield, Lynn, 58, 61
Royal veil length, 103

Satin, 101
Schiffli lace, 99
Seating
    at reception, 240-241
    by ushers, 53
Service, styles of table
    American, 245
    buffet, 243, 246
    English, 247
    family, 246-247
    French, 246
    good stations, 243,247
    hand service, 247
    reception, 247
    Russian, 246
Seton, Andrea Eginton, 256
Shantung fabric, 100
Sheath bridal silhouette, 91
Shower, bridal and parties, 77-86
    bachelor party, 84-85
    bridesmaids' party, 83-84
    gifts, 81-83
    history, 78-79